THE NEGROLAND OF THE ARABS

THE NEGROLAND
OF THE ARABS
examined and explained;

OR

An Inquiry into the
Early History and Geography of
CENTRAL AFRICA

WILLIAM DESBOROUGH COOLEY

SECOND EDITION

With a Bibliographical Introduction by
JOHN RALPH WILLIS

FRANK CASS & CO. LTD.
1966

First published by J. Arrowsmith in 1841

This edition published by
Frank Cass & Co., Ltd.
10 Woburn Walk, London W.C.1

First edition 1841
Second edition 1966

Printed in Great Britain by
Thomas Nelson (Printers) Ltd., London and Edinburgh

BIBLIOGRAPHICAL INTRODUCTION

by

JOHN RALPH WILLIS

FOREWORD

W. D. Cooley's indefatigable spirit of inquiry led him into the diverse fields of geography, mathematics, and linguistics. For his geographical contributions he was made a Fellow of the Royal Geographical Society. Although acknowledged the first to deal in a scientific spirit with questions later solved by actual observation, his investigations sometimes led him to unscientific conclusions. He died (1883) disavowing the existence of snow-capped mountains in Equatorial Africa—this, despite the startling discoveries of Rebmann and Krapf. He underestimated the extent of the Zambezi river and misconstrued the relationship between Lakes Tanganyika and Nyasa. But these views in no way lessened the merit of his greatest work on Africa, *The Negroland of the Arabs*. Indeed this work has remained one of the few of its era which has measured up to the requirements of modern scholarship. Cooley's identifications of place names from the medieval Arab geographers and historians have, for the greater part, gone unchallenged by later authorities, and the *Negroland* has formed a basis for all succeeding investigation.

JOHN RALPH WILLIS

London,
August, 1965

BIBLIOGRAPHY

THE following bibliography will indicate the considerable amount of geographical and historical material published since the first appearance of Cooley's *Negroland.* Readers requiring a more detailed list of works should consult Raymond Mauny's *Tableau Géographique de l'Ouest Africain au Moyen Age d'Aprés les Sources Écrites, la Tradition et l'Archéologie,* Dakar, 1961, the best general introduction to the subject.

ABBREVIATIONS: BCEHSAOF Bulletin du Comité d'Études Historiques et Scientifiques de l'Afrique Occidentale Française; Bulletin de l'I.F.A.N. Bulletin de l'Institut Français d'Afrique Noire.

I *GENERAL STUDIES*

Barth, Heinrich, *Travels and Discoveries in Northern and Central Africa,* 5 vols., 1857. Centenary Edition, 3 vols. 1965.

Bates, Oric, *The Eastern Libyans,* 1914. See bibliography.

Béraud-Villars, J., *L'Empire de Gao,* 1942.

Beazley, C. R., *The Dawn of Modern Geography,* 3 vols., 1906 (reprint, 1949).

Bovill, E. W., *Caravans of the Old Sahara,* 1933.

Davidson, Basil, *Old Africa Rediscovered,* 1959.

Delafosse, M., *Haut-Sénégal-Niger,* 3 vols., 1912.

Fage, J. D., *An Atlas of African History,* 1958.

Fage, J. D., *Ghana*, 1959.

Gautier, E. F., *Le Passé de l'Afrique du Nord,* 1937.

Julien, C. A., *Histoire de l'Afrique du Nord,* 2 vols., 1952 (2nd ed. rev. R. Le Tourneau). See vol. II.

Lebeuf, J. P., Detourbet, A. Masson, *La Civilisation du Tchad,* 1950.

Marquart, J., *Die Benin-Sammlung des Reichsmuseums für Völkerkunde in Leiden,* 1913. Contains extracts from Arabic texts.

Monteil, C., *Djenné*, 1932.

Palmer, Sir H. R., *The Bornu Sahara and Sudan,* 1936.

Rodd, Sir F. R., *People of the Veil,* 1926.

Roncière, C. de la, *La découverte de l'Afrique au moyen âge* ("Mémoires de la Société Royale de Géographie d'Égypte," V, VI, & XIII), 1924–27.

Rouch, J., *Contribution à l'histoire des Songhay* (*Mémoires de l'I.F.A.N.*, no. 29), 1953.

Tilho, J., *Documents Scientifiques de la Mission Tilho* (1906–09), 5 vols., 1910–14.

Trimingham, J. S., *A History of Islam in West Africa,* 1962.

Urvoy, Y., *Petit atlas ethno-demographique du Soudan,* 1942.

Urvoy, Y., *Histoire de l'Empire du Bornu,* (*Mémoires de l'I.F.A.N.*, no. 7), 1949.

II *ARAB GEOGRAPHERS AND HISTORIANS*

Al-Bakrī (d. 1094), *al-Masālik wa'l-Mamālik* (tr. MacGukin de Slane as *Description de l'Afrique Septentrionale,* 2nd ed., 1913; Arabic text, 2nd ed., 1910). The de Slane editions are only fragments of the original. For a short biographical account and bibliography consult E. Lévi-Provençal's article in the *Encyclopedia of Islam,* new edition.

Al-Mas'ūdī (d. 956), *Murūj al-dhahab wa-Ma'ādin al-jawāhir* (ed. & tr. C. Barbier de Meynard & Pavet de Courteille as *Les Prairies d'or,* 9 vols., 1861–77). This edition combines Arabic text with French translation.

Al- 'Umarī (d. 1349), *Masālik al-abṣār fī mamālik al-amṣār* (I, *L'Afrique, moins l'Égypte,* tr. M. Gaudefroy-Demombynes, 1927). Incomplete translation containing chapters on: "Abyssinie, Soudan, Maghreb, et Andalousie."

Al-Qalqashandī (d. 1418), *Kitāb Ṣubḥ al-A'shā fī Ṣinā'āt al-Inshā'* (publication of the Dār al-Kutub al-Khadīwīya, Cairo), 14 vols., 1913–19. See vol. VIII, pp. 116–18, for Kanem-Bornu, and vol. V, for Ghāna & Māli.

Al-Ya 'qūbī (d. after 891), *Kitāb al-Buldān* (ed. & tr. M. J. de Goeje, 1860, 2nd ed., 1892 in vol. VII of *Bibliotheca geographorum Arabicorum,* 8 vols., 1885–1927; *trad. franç.,* G. Wiet, *Textes et Traductions d'auteurs Orientales,* I, 1937). This work has not survived in its entirety.

Ibn 'Abd al-Ḥakam (d. 871), *Futūḥ Miṣr wa'l-Maghrib* (Arabic text, C. C. Torrey, *The 'Futūḥ Miṣr' of Ibn 'Abd al-Ḥakam . . ., Yale Oriental Series, Research,* vol. III, 1922; portions concerning N. Africa & Spain translated by A. Gateau as *Conquête de l'Afrique du Nord et de l'Espagne, Bibliothèque arabe-française,* t. II, 1948); See R. Brunschvig, "Ibn 'Abd al-Ḥakam . . ." *Annales de l'Institut d'Études Orientales,* Algiers VI, 1942-7, pp. 108-55.

Ibn Abī Zar' (d. 1326), *al-Anīs al-muṭrib (bi-raud(at) al-Qirṭās fī akhbār mulūk al-Maghrib wa-ta'rīkh madīnat Fās* (see C. Brockelmann's *Geschichte der Arabischen Litteratur,* G.II, 240). The Arabic text was edited by C. J. Tornberg, 1839 (see J. S. Trimingham, *op. cit.,* p. 21, note) and there is a French translation by A. Beamier, *Roudh el Kartas, Histoire des souverains du Maghreb et annales de la ville de Fès,* Paris, 1860.

Ibn Baṭṭūṭa, (d. 1377), *Tuḥfat al-Nuẓẓār fī Gharā' ib al-Amṣār wa* 'Ajā'-*ib al-Asfār* (ed. & tr. C. Defrémery & R. B. Sanguinetti, 5 vols., 3rd ed., 1893, see vol. IV; the greater part of his Western Sudan journey is contained in *Ibn Battúta Travels in Asia and Africa,* selections tr. & ed. by Sir H. A. R. Gibb, 1929; new edition, of which 2 vols. have appeared, in preparation by same author).

N'Di aye, A., "Sur la transcription des vocables africains par Ibn Baththutha," *Notes Africains,* no. 38, April 1948, pp. 26–7, no. 41, January 1949, p. 31.

Ibn Ḥawqal (d. 977), *Kitāb al-Masālik wa' l-Mamālik Sūrat al-arḍ,* portion relating in part to N. Africa, ed. & tr. M. J. de Goeje, 1860, 2nd ed. J. H. Kramers, 1938, in vol. II of *Bibliotheca geographorum Arabicorum*; also tr. by de Slane as *Description de l'Afrique* in the *Journal Asiatique,* 1842; *cf.* Sir William Ouseley's *The Geography of Ebn Haukal,* 1800.

Ibn Khaldūn (d. 1406), *Kitāb al- 'ibar wa-dīwān al-mubtada' wa'l-khabar* . . . (Būlāq, 1867, 7 vols.; parts on N. Africa translated by de Slane as *Histoire des Berberes,* new edition, Paul Casanova, 4 vols., 1925–56; the introduction, *Muqaddima,* tr. & ed. F. Rosenthal, 3 vols., 1958).

Ibn Sa'īd (d. 1274), . . . *al-Mughrib fī ḥulā (maḥāsin ahl) al-maghrib* (see C. Brockelmann's *Geschichte der Arabischen Litteratur* G.I, 337). The chronicle of this philologist has been only partially preserved. He is often quoted by Ibn Khaldūn and Abū'l-Fidā' (d. 1331) (*Taqwīm al-Buldān* ed. J. T. Reinaud & MacGuckin de Slane, 1840; tr. Reinaud, vol. I, *Introduction générale à la géographie des Orientaux,* q.v., vol. II, tr. part I by Reinaud, 1848, tr. part II by St. Guyard, 1883).

Idrīsī (d. 1166), *Nuzhat al-mushtāq fī' khtirāq al-āfāq* (African & Spanish parts ed. & tr. R. Dozy & de Goeje as *Description de l'Afrique et de l'Espagne,* 1866, reprint in preparation). See V. Monteil, "L'oeuvre d'Idrisi," *Bulletin de l'I.F.A.N.,* 1939, pp. 837–57.

Latreille, M., *Recherches géographiques sur l'Afrique centrale d'après les écrits d'Edrisi et de Léon l'Africain, comparés avec les relations modernes,* 1824, 30 pp.

Leo Africanus (d. after 1526): the best edition of this writer's work is *Description de l'Afrique,* edited & copiously annotated by A. Épaulard, T. Monod, H. Lhote, & R. Mauny, 2 vols., 1956, but see J. Pory edition for the Hakluyt Society, *History and Description of Africa,* 3 vols., 1896, reprint, 1963. See also Sir H. R. Palmer, "The Kingdom of Gaoga of Leo Africanus," *Journal of the African Society,* xxix, 1929–30, pp. 280–284 & 350–369.

Maqrīzī (d. 1442): several of his works have important information on the Western Sudan (see J. S. Trimingham, *A History of Islam in West Africa,* index, 1962 & C. Brocklemann's article in the *Encyclopedia of Islam,* first edition).

Mauny, R., "L'Afrique Occidentale d'après les auteurs arabes anciens (666–977)," *Notes Africaines,* no. 40, Nov. 1948, pp. 6–7.

Mauny, R., "L'Ouest Africain chez les géographes arabes du Moyen Age," *Comptes rendus de la Conférence Internationale des Africanistes de l'Ouest,* Santa Isabel, 1951, vol. II, pp. 503–508.

Yāqūt al-Rūmī (d. 1229), *Mu 'jam al-Buldān* (see rev. Cairo edition, 10 vols., 1906–1907; also tr. & ed. by F. Wüstenfeld as *Jacut's Geographisches Wörterbuch,* 2nd edition, 6 vols., 1924). See Yāqūt for material from al-Muhallabī's *al-'Azīzī* (written *c.* 985), which has not survived.

Yūsuf Kamāl (Prince), *Monumenta Cartographica Africae et Aegypti,* 5 vols., 1926–51. Indispensible for the non-Arabist, containing relevant passages from many of above authorities, Arabic text with parallel French translation.

III *CITIES AND STATES*

GHĀNA AND MĀLI: Bonnel de Mézières, A., "Recherches sur l'emplacement de Ghana et de Takrour," Paris, *Mémoires de la Académie d'Inscriptions et Belles Lettres,* 1920, pp. 227–73; Delafosse, M., "La Question de Ghana et la Mission Bonnel de Mézieres," *Annuaire et Mémoires du Comité d'Études Historiques et Scientifiques de l'Afrique Occidentale française,* 1916, pp. 40–61; Delafosse, M., "Le Gâna et le Mali et l'emplacement de leurs capitales," *BCEHSAOF,* 1924, pp. 479–542; Desplagnes, L., "Note sur l'emplacement des ruines de Ganna ou Gannata, ancienne capitale soudanaise antérieure à l'Islam," *Bulletin de la Société de Géographie de l'Afrique Occidentale française,* no. 4, December 31, 1907, pp. 298–301; Fage, J. D., "Ancient Ghana: A Review of the Evidence," *Transactions of the Historical Society of Ghana,* III, no. 2, 1957; Gaillard, M., "Niani, ancienne capitale de l'empire mandingue," *BCEHSAOF,* 1923, pp. 620–36; Hervé, H., "Niani, ex-capitale de l'Empire mandingue," *Notes Africaines,* no. 82, April 1959, pp. 51–5; Laforgue, P.," Notes sur

Aoudaghost, Ancienne Capitale des Berberes Lemtouna," *Bulletin de l'I.F.A.N.,* 1940, pp. 217–36. Mauny, R., "The Question of Ghana," *Africa,* XXIV, June 1954, pp. 200–13. Mauny, R., "Les Ruines de Tegdaoust et le Question d'Aoudaghost," *Notes Africaines,* no. 48, October 1950, pp. 107–9; Mauny, R., "État actuel de la question de Ghana," *Bulletin de l'I.F.A.N.,* 1951, pp. 463–75; Monteil, C., "Les Empires du Mali," *BCEHSAOF,* XII, 1929, pp. 291–447. Monteil, C., "Les 'Ghana' des Géographes Arabes et des Européens," *Hespéris,* XXXVIII, 1951, pp. 441–452; Montrat, M., "Notice sur l'emplacement de l'ancienne capitale du Mali," *Notes Africaines,* no. 79, July 1958, pp. 90–3; Vidal, J., "Au sujet de l'emplacement de Mali (ou Melli), capitale de l'ancien empire mandingue," *BCEHSAOF,* 1923, pp. 251–268, "Le mystère de Ghana," pp. 512–24, "Le véritable emplacement de Mali," pp. 606–19.

GAO: Mauny, R., "Notes d'Archéologie au subject de Gao," *Bulletin de l'I.F.A.N.,* 1951, pp. 837–52; Mauny, R., "Notes d'archéologie sur Tombouktou," *Bulletin de l'I.F.A.N.,* 1952, pp. 899–918. Sauvaget, J., "Notes préliminaires sur les épitaphes royales de Gao," *Revue des Études Islamiques,* 1948, pp. 5–12, "Les épitaphes royales de Gao," *Al-Andalus,* XIV, 1949, pp. 123–41 & *Bulletin de l'I.F.A.N.,* 1950, pp. 418–40; Viré, M. M., "Notes sur trois épitaphes royales de Gao," *Bulletin de l'I.F.A.N.,* 1958, pp. 368–76, "Stèles funéraires musulmanes soudano-sahariennes," *Bulletin de l'I.F.A.N.,* 1959, pp. 459–500.

KANEM-BORNU: Bivar, A. D. H., & Shinnie, P. L., "Old Kanuri Capitals," *Journal of African History,* III, no. 1, 1962, pp. 1–11.

TAGHĀZA: Chudeau, R., "Taoudenni et Teghazza d'après les notes du Capit. Grosdemange," *Bulletin du Comité de l'Afrique Française,* XX, 1910, pp. 13–16; Monod, T., "Nouvelles remarques sur Teghaza," *Bulletin de l'I.F.A.N.,* 1940, pp. 248–50.

AWLĪL: Monteil, C., "L'ile d'Aulil d'Idrisi," *Notes Africaines,* no. 48, October 1950, pp. 128–130.

SIJILMĀSA: Terasse, H., "Note sur les ruines de Sijilmassa," *Revue Africaine,* II, no. 368–369, 1936, pp. 581–89.

JOHN RALPH WILLIS

LONDON, 1965

THE NEGROLAND

OF THE ARABS

EXAMINED AND EXPLAINED;

OR,

AN INQUIRY INTO THE

EARLY HISTORY AND GEOGRAPHY

OF

CENTRAL AFRICA.

BY

WILLIAM DESBOROUGH COOLEY.

LONDON:

PRINTED BY JAMES HOLMES, TOOK'S COURT.

PUBLISHED BY J. ARROWSMITH, 10, SOHO SQUARE.

1841.

TO SEÑOR

DON PASCUAL DE GAYANGOS.

MY DEAR GAYANGOS,

THE following Essay owes its origin wholly to the extracts from the writings of Ibn Khaldún and Ibn Baṭúṭah, which you had the kindness to communicate to me. Not only did you occasion the present developement of my speculations, but you have also at all times cheerfully aided me in the researches to which they gave birth; you have placed at my disposal, as it were, your perfect knowledge of the Arabic language, and, from the abundance of your learning, have in some measure made good my deficiency. To whom, then, can this little work be dedicated so justly, as to you? Nor, while acknowledging my obligations, can I forego the pleasure afforded by such an opportunity of expressing towards you the friendship and esteem of

Yours sincerely,

WILLIAM DESBOROUGH COOLEY.

London, March 3, 1841.

PREFACE.

THE following Essay has for its object to establish the early geography of Central Africa on a solid basis. It aims at offering a clear and well-grounded explanation of the geographical descriptions of Negroland, transmitted to us by Arab writers; and, by thus connecting the past with the present, at giving an increased value to the historical information derived from the same sources. The attainment of that end will throw a steady light on the past condition of a country now awakening a general interest. It will enable us to trace some important political revolutions; to discern the nations which have stood forth politically eminent, and to estimate correctly, by means of a lengthened and authentic retrospect, the progress of civilization in Africa.

The task here undertaken has more of novelty in it than may be at first suspected. Hitherto no attempt whatever has been made to explain the Arab geography of Negroland by treating it as a whole, and as the immediate subject of investigation. Yet no department of the wide field of literature stands more in need of critical labour, or appears more justly entitled to it. The Arabs in the Middle Ages were copious and circumstantial writers, though neither profound nor exact. Geography was one of their favourite studies. The interests of trade and religious zeal led them across the deserts of Northern Africa to Negroland, of which they have left us accounts bearing in every lineament the expression of unaffected sincerity. Yet such has been the difficulty found in recognizing the places described in those accounts, that, up to this day, scarcely any addition to our positive knowledge of Negroland has been derived from the writings of the Arabs.

Ibn S'aíd, a writer of the thirteenth century, has enumerated thirteen nations of Blacks, extending across Africa, from Ghánah in the west, to the Bojá on the shores of the Red Sea in the east. Yet it is not till we arrive at the tenth of these, or Kánem, that we are able to identify satisfactorily the nomenclature of Ibn S'aíd with that of modern geography. The first nine nations towards the west, or nearly three-fourths of the whole, remain undetermined.

The Arab geography of Africa lies, at present, a large but confused heap of materials, into which modern writers occasionally dip their hands, each selecting what appears to serve his purpose, and adapting it to his views by an interpretation as narrow and partial as his mode of inquiry. Modern geographers—D'Anville and Rennell not excepted—have allowed fancied resemblances of sound to lead them far away from fact and the straight path of investigation. They have, for example, unanimously assumed the Kanó of the present day to be the Ghánah of past ages. The disorder introduced into the early geography of Central Africa by this false method of proceeding, has deprived it of all its value. It seems incapable of combining with the results of modern discovery; and instead of the harmony which ought to subsist between our present information and the ample accounts of Negroland written five or six centuries ago, we find in almost every application of the latter, the jarring consequences of false assumptions.

To give a new value to such confused materials, we must have recourse to a new and improved method of treating them.

The course here followed is, to examine the Arab authors of greatest value, and to develope, as completely as possible, the information found in them, their meaning being collected altogether from internal evidence, and without any regard to extrinsic systems. Where their statements are clear, natural, and consistent, no attempt has been made to interfere with or strain them by arbitrary conjectures. Where, on the other hand, they are obscure, absurd, or contradictory, care has been taken to inquire,—1st, What were the sources or channels of the author's information? 2ndly, How far it must be taken in strictness, or may claim the latitude allowed to the language of ordinary discourse? 3rdly, The state of knowledge, and prevalent geographical systems in the writer's time? 4thly, What portions may be looked upon as original or authentic, and what as founded on inference or surmise?—The point of greatest difficulty, and which demands the utmost care and perspicacity, is to distinguish between the language of experience and that of system; to separate the original information from the supplementary additions made to it, for the purpose of filling up or rounding the description, or of reconciling it with theoretical conceptions.

In all parts of the world, and in every age, the human mind moves in a constant cycle. In like stages of its progress it occupies similar positions, and goes through the same round of error. This truth is exemplified in the history of Geography, as well as in that of every other branch of human knowledge. The corrections made in our maps of Africa during the last three centuries; those made by Ptolemy in the geography of the same quarter of the globe, written by Marinus Tyrius; and those of which the great Alexandrian himself stands in need, are nearly all reducible to one common rule. The errors to which systematical geography tends, while it is not as yet founded on science, are so fully shown by experience, that we can safely derive from our knowledge of them a principle of rectification, applicable to all the materials of unscientific geography, presented to our notice, and obviously needing correction. The endeavour to trace errors according to fixed analogies, will at least lead us from mere conjecture towards a rule of reason.

The most vexatious and frequently recurring hindrance in researches of the kind here undertaken, arises from the defects of the Arabic written character, and the uncritical servility of Arab copyists and compilers. In Arabic writing, some of the characters closely resemble one another, and are distinguished only by diacritic points: the vowels likewise are chiefly indicated by points, which, like those of the former kind, are often wholly omitted. Hence it follows, that proper names, the correct reading of which cannot be inferred from the context, easily sink, when written in such ambiguous characters, from corruption to corruption, till at last they altogether cease to be recognizable. Misnomers arising in this way were perhaps often adopted in discourse, till, in process of time, they became authorized by usage. Uncertainty with respect to the true reading of proper names, besides being in itself a source of great perplexity, has the ill effect of encumbering the truth with much preliminary discussion of an apparently trivial kind. Nor are our difficulties with respect to proper names confined to the writings of the Arabs. In some parts of Africa, different races are so commingled, that five or six languages may be heard spoken within a narrow extent of territory. Travellers arriving in such a country from different quarters, and associating with different portions of the population, will naturally report in different ways the names of places. If Europeans, they variously represent, each according to the genius of his own language, articulations which, being strange to their organs, they did not invariably seize correctly. Names have been also transferred from one language to another, without due regard to the sound originally sought to be represented. Here, then, are abundant sources of confusion, which, so far, at least, as it involves the genius and construction of African languages, we are not always in a condition to clear up. Yet it is necessary, as we proceed, to endeavour to distinguish between the more and the less doubtful; and if any one should feel surprised at the attention occasionally bestowed in the following pages on proper names, let him only reflect, that the errors arising from the neglect of so many inevitable causes of variance, would at least equal what may ensue from even the least skilful discussion of them.

It would have been easy to lengthen the list of Arab authors here made use of; but little would have been gained for Geography by reference to works equally deficient in judgment and originality. The authors chiefly relied on are, El Bekrí, Ibn Khaldún, and Ibn Baṭúṭah. El Idrísí is analysed in some passages, chiefly for the sake of explaining certain discrepancies between him and the first-named writer, and to estimate the weight due to his authority. The conjectures scattered through the following pages are much fewer than the nature of the subject and the course of investigation would have permitted; but it was thought advisable to keep conjectures within bounds, even where they could not have interfered with the reasoning. Reserve and circumspection are especially necessary for an author whose conclusions differ widely from those of his precursors in the same field of inquiry, and who aims at deciding definitively questions which have long divided the judgments of the learned. Reference to the systems of recent authors has been, in general, avoided, lest the frequent recurrence of the language of refutation might give the whole an air of controversy. Pains have been also taken to abridge whatever was not strictly geographical, the object here aimed at being properly the consideration of geographical questions, the careful and satisfactory discussion of which demands a special treatise.

The mode here adopted of writing the Arabic names, is fully explained in the Journal of the Royal Geographical Society, vol. VII. p. 245; but in its application will probably be found much unsteadiness and imperfection, arising partly from the want of familiarity with it, and partly from the difficulty of setting exact bounds to the employment of a foreign orthography, which jars disagreeably with the necessary reference to the orthography of our modern travellers. The attempt at a systematic reform of the mode of writing African names, has been avoided, and therewith the alternative also, of either multiplying without end the subordinate topics of discussion, or else of allowing much hypothesis to steal in under the mask of precision.

In conclusion, it may be remarked, that the attempt here made, however successful it may be deemed—and it cannot be denied that it broaches some truths, and discloses a new and logical method of treating an interesting subject—is yet but a sketch, which remains to be filled up, after a careful examination of the numerous Arabic MSS. preserved in the public libraries here and abroad, by some one better qualified for that labour, and enjoying fairer opportunities than the writer of these pages.

CONTENTS.

KÚGHAH, KÁGHÓ, KAÚKAÚ, KARKAR.

LEMLEM, REMREM, DEMDEM, EL-LÍMIYÍN,

NEGROLAND DIVIDED INTO NATIONS.

POSTSCRIPT.

REMARKS ON HOUSSA.

CORRECTIONS.

Page 14, note 27—for Moallakah read Maḳámah.
Page 60, note 103—for A'walílí read Awalílí.

THE

NEGROLAND

OF THE ARABS.

INTRODUCTION.

NATURE has marked out, in a plain and peremptory manner, the chief lines of communication between the maritime regions of North Africa and the fertile Interior beyond the great desert. The Oasis, or habitable tract of Fezzán, south of Tripoli, projects far into the barren waste, and a journey of not more than forty days conducts thence to Kánem or Bornú. In the west, a route of equal length connects the last traces of cultivation at the back of Atlas, with the Great River of Negroland, where, winding in a long circuit towards the north, it seems to drive back desolation, and narrows the limits of the desert. The two routes here described, are those chiefly frequented at the present day by caravans proceeding to Central Africa; and the preference given to them is due to their combining such advantages of convenience and security, as must have constituted them the chief routes in all ages.

The first of these, or the road between Fezzán and the interior, may be presumed to have been frequented by the ancients. If we assume that commerce spread westward from Egypt, or if we fix our eyes on Augila or the Greek colony of Cyrene, the eastern route will certainly seem entitled to be the channel of the earliest intercourse with the Blacks. But the discussion of such questions does not lie within the scope of our present inquiry; and it will be here sufficient to observe, that so far as the Arabs were concerned, the western route, though last reached, was the most frequently trodden and most diligently explored. The stream of Arab invasion in Northern Africa flowed rapidly to the west, till accumulating between the shores of the Ocean and Atlas, it pressed on the Berber clans inhabiting all the fertile recesses of this range of mountains. Continual wars thence ensued, in the course of which the discomfited party always fled to the desert, wherein they wandered to the borders of Negroland.

It is by the western route that we have derived, through Arab writers, the amplest and earliest accounts of Central Africa. For the Arabs in Spain who cultivated letters maintained a constant intercourse with their rude but active brethren of Western Barbary, whom trade and warfare alike occasionally impelled to visit the countries beyond the desert. In the beginning of the eleventh century of our era, the hills on the south side of Wád Nún and Daráh, or the northern portion of the western desert, were occupied by the Lumtúnah, a tribe of the Zenágah.[1] Separated from them by an uninhabited tract, were the Benú Goddálah of the same nation, whose territory, comprising the southern zone of the Ṣaḥrá, extended eastward from the sea shore to the country of the Blacks.[2] The more sterile tracts of the desert in the interior, within the limits possessed by the Zenágah, were abandoned

---

[1] Wád Nún is also called by early writers Núl, or Núl el akṣa. Daráh دَرَعه is also written Diráh دِرعه (MS. B.M. fol. 101)—Lumtúnah لمتونه—The Berber name Zenághah زَناغه was corrupted by the Arabs, as Ibn Khaldún informs us, into Ṣinhájah صنهاجه, pronounced in the west Ṣinhágah.

[2] Goddála, so pronounced, though written by El Bekrí Joddála جدّاله (MS. B.M. fol. 106); by Ibn Khaldún and others, Godálah ݣداله.

to the wandering tribe of the Benú Masúfah, by their more powerful brethren near the coast.[3] These three tribes, inflamed with religious zeal, to which their intestine feuds had given a martial character, shaped their course northward, and being united under the name of Al Morábiṭún, or Champions of the Faith, they subjugated the fertile countries on both sides of the southern Atlas, and founded, in 1073, the empire and city of Morocco. The Al Morábiṭún, or Morabites, subsequently extended their sway into Spain, in the history of which country they figure under the name of Almoravides. But long before they carried their arms into Europe, they corresponded intimately with the polished courts of Mohammedan Spain; and while they had not yet quite relinquished the desert, nor forgotten their acquaintance with the frontiers of Negroland, they communicated their information to the inquisitive, and, for that age, well instructed Spanish Arabs. The age immediately preceding the foundation of Morocco is that in which we should accordingly expect to find the most valuable accounts of the Western Desert, and of the Negro kingdoms contiguous to it. The events of that period were calculated to bring within the reach of literary activity, full, fresh, and authentic information respecting the interior of Western Africa. It is fortunate for us, therefore, that we possess an account of that country written in the very age referred to, by one who resided at the most accomplished court in Spain; whose station in society and official rank afforded him the amplest means of satisfying his curiosity; and whose perspicuity and good sense entitle him to a distinguished place among Arab writers. The author here alluded to, Abú 'Obeïdi-llah Abdullah el Ḳorṭoby, was son of the independent ruler of Huelva. He resided chiefly in Cordova, at that time the centre of Arab refinement, and filled the highest offices in that kingdom. His account of Negroland, entitled 'Kitábu-l-mesálek wa-l-memálek,' or the Book of Roads and Realms, was written in the year of the Hijra 460, or A. D. 1067, just fourteen years after the first rise of the Morabites, and six

[3] Benú Masúfah بنو مسوفة.

before the foundation of Morocco. We shall therefore take El Bekrí as our guide while endeavouring to determine the true position of Ghánah, in his age the principal kingdom of Negroland.[5]

---

[5] For an account of this valuable author, see the recently published History of the Mohammedan Dynasties in Spain, by Don Pascual de Gayangos, p. 324. The excellent MS. in the library of the British Museum (No. 9577) there described, shall be here briefly cited as MS. B.M. A translation of El Bekrí's Book of Roads and Realms, by M. Quatremère, has appeared in the 12th volume of the Collection entitled 'Notices et Extraits des MSS. de la Bibliothèque du Roi.' But the Parisian MS. is so deficient in points, that the translator, notwithstanding his learning and acuteness, has not always been able to divine the true reading. A fragment of the same work, containing what relates to Ghánah, has been translated by M. Jaubert, to whom it was sent from Barbary, and inserted in the 2nd volume of the 'Recueil des Voyages et Mémoires,' &c. published by the Société de Géographie in Paris. Wherever this extract, which is taken from a MS. of inferior authority, is quoted alone in the following pages, the reader may understand that the readings so adopted agree in characters with the readings found in the MS. B.M., and have in addition the vowel points.

GHA'NAH—Aúdaghost—Aúlíl.

Previous to the foundation of Morocco, all the trade of Negroland with Western Barbary was directed towards Sijilmésah, a town on the eastern side of Atlas, eight or ten days from Fás or Fez, and in the district which is now called Táfílélt.[1] From Sijilmésah, a two months' journey southward conducted to the nearest kingdom of the Blacks, which was that called Ghánah.[2] But in propriety of speech Ghánah

---

[1] Chénier (Recherches sur les Maures, tom. III. pp. 16 and 79) was the first to pronounce, Walckenaer (Recherches sur l'Afrique Septentrionale, 1822, p. 285) the first to prove, the identity of Sijilmésah سجلماسة with Táfílélt تافيلالت. The arguments of the latter amount to demonstration, and need no reinforcement. Yet we may be permitted to add, that all the Arab writers, without exception, make Sijilmésah contiguous to Daráh درعة; and that the uncritical Marmol, although he subjoins to his description of Sijilmésah (vol. III. fol. 8) an account also of Táfílélt, denuded of every circumstance which could help to determine its geographical position, yet in copying Leo's list of the provinces of Numidia, omits Sijilmésah, and substitutes for it Táfílélt (Leo Africanus, pt. I. c. 5. in Ramusio, 1554, vol. I. fol. 1 v, Marmol, I. fol. 12). The name Táfílélt seems to have come into use with the rise of the dynasty of the Fílélí sherífs. The tribe, ennobled by events, gave its name to the country in which it was established. M. Gråberg af Hemsö, therefore (Specchio di Marocco, 1834, p. 65), who refuses his assent to M. Walckenaer's conclusions, and separates Táfílélt from Sijilmésah for reasons of comparatively little weight, cannot certainly vindicate his mode of using the former of these names, by showing that it occurs in the pages of any historian, native or foreign, anterior to the sixteenth century. The Fílélí tribe or family are however of ancient standing, for Ibn Baṭúṭah informs us that at Kaúkaú, in Negroland, in A. D. 1353, he became acquainted with the fakíh or doctor, Mohammed the Fílélí الفيلالي.

[2] Ghánah غَانَة and غَانَةَ (MS. B.M.). The final *hé* ة of the Arabs, when pointed ة, is pronounced as *t* before a vowel; غَانَة and غَانَةَ therefore, when not immediately followed by consonants, are read Ghánaṭ and Ghánaṭa. But the suppression of the *t* in this instance seems to be due altogether to the analogies of the Arabic language, and probably was not always imitated by the

was the title of the king, whose dominion, anterior to the rise of the Al Morábiṭún or Morabites, extended to Aúdaghost, a town on the southern border of the great desert, and containing a Berber population.[3] Driven from Aúdaghost, the negro king fixed his residence at Aúkár, fifteen days' journey southwestward from the former place, and not far from the great river of the interior, called by Arab writers the Nile of the Blacks.[4] But the new capital, as well as the kingdom, was still generally known by the name of Ghánah.

A desert of forty days' journey in extent lay between Aúdaghost and Támedelt,[5] a town of Sús el Akṣa, on the verge of the desert, and eleven days from Sijilmésah. The two months' journey between Ghánah and Sijilmésah, would, if literally interpreted, place the capital of the Blacks forty-nine days distant from Támedelt. But where could a route of forty-nine days southward from the borders of Sús el Akṣa

---

Berbers, in which language *t* is a frequent termination. Hence it is not surprising that in an extract from El Bekrí, sent from Tripoli by M. Gråberg af Hemsö, to M. Jaubert (Recueil, &c. par la Soc. de Géogr. tom. II. 1825), we should find Ghánat غَانَتْ constantly written instead of Ghánah غانة. The importance of this remark will appear hereafter.

[3] The Arabic *wa* و when it begins a word, is a consonant, like our *w*. Hence, when the Arabs would write a name beginning with a long *o* or *u*, they are obliged to prefix an aleph ا to the wa و to preserve to the latter its vocal function; thus اودغست, اوليل, اوكار, would be written to express Odaghost or Udagost, Olíl or Ulíl, Okár or Ukár. The áú او may be also intended for a diphthong. But it must be observed that the prefixed aleph in the Berber language is a sign of case, and may have other offices; there is some temerity therefore in excluding the form Awadagost, and in reading Berber names according to the analogies of a foreign language.

[4] Not. et Extr. p. 642. The reasons for concluding that Aúkár lay to the south-west of Aúdaghost, will be shown hereafter. El Bekrí states more than once that Ghánah was the king's title. Not. et Extr. pp. 630 and 642.

[5] Támedelt تَلَمَدَلْت (MS. B.M.) is read by M. Quatremère, Tamdoult. Sús el Akṣa, i. e. the remote Sús, is the most southern province of Morocco, on the confines of the desert.

meet the Great River, unless in the vicinity of Tomboktú?[6] This city is distant about two months from Táfílélt, and not more than fifty days from Sús el Akṣa.[7] It owes all its importance to its advanced position, near the very point where the river turns eastward, after repressing the desert in its northerly course, and making its nearest approach to Western Barbary. The advantages of such a position could never have been overlooked while caravans traversed the desolate plains of the interior. The site of Ghánah then, and Tomboktú, being equidistant from Sús el Akṣa, both in a southerly direction from it, and both in the vicinity of the Great River, which, within the distance of fifty days from Sús el Akṣa, washes the desert during only a short part of its course, cannot have been far asunder. This brief argument is in reality unanswerable. Within the assigned time, a caravan travelling at the ordinary pace, could reach the Great River nowhere but in the vicinity of Tomboktú. The site of Aúkár then being near Tomboktú, Aúdaghost fifteen days distant from it towards the north-east, must have been situate in the same tract as the modern town or encampment of Mabrúk.[8] Thus the first view of the routes to the chief towns of the ancient Ghánah suggests the approximate positions of those towns. Let their positions be assumed accordingly, so as to give distinctness to our conceptions, while we follow, step by step, the routes to them across the desert; and the examination of these routes in all their particulars will, in turn, illustrate and confirm our assumptions, if they be correct.

---

6 The routes to Ghánah and Aúdaghost went southward, according to Abulfedá, but this expression need not be strictly understood. (Abulfedá's Geography, translated by Reiske in Büsching's Magazin, vol. IV. 212, v. 354). Tomboktú is here spelt as dictated by Ibn Baṭúṭah. The river of Negroland, which, in the successive parts of its course is named Joliba, Issa, Quorra, &c., and which theory and false learning have styled the Niger, will be generally denominated, throughout the following pages, *the Great River.*

7 Caillié reckoned fifty-seven days of actual travelling between Tomboktú and Táfílélt.

8 Mabrúk is said by some (Itinerary of Ḥáj Ḳásim, in Walckenaer, Rech. p. 426) to be eleven days, by others (Mohammed of Tripoli, in the Quarterly Review, No. 45, p. 231) fifteen from Tomboktú.

The position of Támedelt, the starting point of the caravans to Negroland, must be in the first place determined. That town is stated to have been five days westward (or, we must rather suppose, south of westward) from Daràh, and six days south-eastward from Iklí, the capital of Sús, which town, situate on a river flowing northward, was two days from Mésah and five from Wád Nún. Now the capital of Daràh was five days distant from Sijilmésah, which was nine ordinary journeys from Fez.[9] Támedelt was therefore twenty days from Fez, by the road on the eastern side of the mountains, and it was also six days south-eastward from Iklí, which town must accordingly be so placed within five days of Wád Nún, and two days northward from the river of Mésah, as to allow Támedelt a somewhat westerly bearing from Daràh. These conditions being fulfilled, the position of Támadelt will be nearly in lat. 28° 45′ N., long. 7° 10′ W., and not far from the modern Tatta.[10] The position thus assumed, though not quite free from uncertainty, will yet involve no inaccuracy capable of endangering the argument depending on it.

The starting point being ascertained, there remains no dif-

---

9 Since the intercourse between Fez and Támedelt need not be considered as merely commercial, it would be injudicious to measure the routes between them by the journeys of a loaded caravan. El Bekrí (Not. et Extr. p. 598) reckons eight days' journey between Fez and Sijilmésah, but one of them was a long journey (across the desert of Angad) of sixty miles. Abulfedá makes the distance between these cities to be ten days' journey. We reckon nine days, so as make the whole distance of Fez from Támedelt twenty days' journey, and allow twenty-two geographical miles to each. The bearing of Támedelt from Iklí is said to have been in the direction of the Ḳibla بقبلي (MS. B.M. fol. 105), or temple of Mekkah, towards which the followers of Mohammed turn their faces when they pray. The direction of the Ḳibla is understood in Morocco, according to Windus (Journey to Morocco, p. 49) to mean east by south.

10 The caravans from Sijilmésah to Ghánah, like those to Tomboktú, assembled on the confines of Sús, Daràh, and the desert. Tatta, the gathering place of the merchants going to Tomboktú, as placed by Major Rennell, on information derived from the British consul at Mogadore (Proceedings of the African Assoc. 1810, vol. I. p. 254), is not more than two days distant from the site of Támedelt; and El Harib, the point at which Caillié, travelling northward, quitted the desert, was but four or five days distant from these places.

ficulty in tracing the route to Aúdaghost. The first day's journey from Támedelt conducted to a deep well called Bír el Jemmálín:[11] the second led through a narrow defile. Then for three days the road went over the mountains of Azawwar,[12] strewed with masses of iron-stone. These mountains extend, according to El Bekrí, ten days' journey from the ocean to the road (from Támedelt probably) to Sijilmésah. They are evidently the same chain of mountains which caravans now pass at the distance of six days from Wád Nún. It is apparent also that the road to Aúdaghost must have crossed them at a distance not exceeding ten days' journey from the sea; and therefore could have scarcely inclined towards the east. Three days beyond the mountains was the watering place of Tendefas, and three days further a great well called Weínhílún.[13] Then another three days led to a scanty spring named Tázḳa, or the House.[14] Four days further were the brackish wells of Weítúnán, and after another four days the watering place of Aúkázenta.[15] There ended the hard desert, and the region of loose sand-hills commenced, the passage of which presented the greatest difficulty to the traveller, and was fraught with danger.

---

[11] Bír el Jemmálín بير الجمالين (MS. B.M. fol. 101), the Camel-keepers' well. M. Quatremère (Not. et Extr. p. 612) reads Bír el Ḥammálín, that is, the Porters' well. But as this name occurs in the route from Wádi Daràh, it is fortunate that a pointed MS. enables us to distinguish clearly between those two places, the proximity of which would conduce to the embarrassment likely to result from their being confounded together.

[12] Azawwar أَزَوَّر MS. B.M. fol. 102; Azour in Not. et Extr. p. 613. This name may, with much probability, be read Azawwad ازود, that is, the dry or sterile country.

[13] Tendefas تندفس MS. B.M. fol. 102; Tendefak, Not. et Extr. p. 613. Weínhílún وَيْنْهَيْلُون MS. B.M.; Wirhaloun, Not. et Extr.

[14] Tázḳa تَازقي MS. B.M.; Tarka, Not. et Extr. This word, written *Taskha* by Capt. Lyon (Travels in North Africa, p. 315), is still retained in the dialect of the Tawárik.

[15] Weíṭúnán وَيْطُونَان MS. B.M.—Aúkázenta اوكازَنْت MS. B.M.; Oukarit, Not. et Extr.

The northern limit and general direction of the sandy region of the great desert are marked out with tolerable distinctness in the narratives of some modern travellers. It was on the twenty-fifth day of his journey from Wád Nún to Tomboktú that Sidi Hamed entered the region of drifting sand.[16] This must have been somewhere between the twenty-third and twenty-fourth parallels of latitude. In the same line, or twenty-two days from El Harib, between Tatta and Darȧh, Caillié left the sand-hills on his journey from Tomboktú northwards.[17] Laing, on his way from Twát to Tomboktú, entered the sands in lat. 23° 56′ N.; and Scott crossed a similar tract, eleven days' journey in extent, apparently from the twenty-first to the twenty-third parallel inclusive, and not far from the ocean.[18]

[16] Sidi Hamed, leaving Wád Nún, went six days round the mountains towards the south, that is, he cleared the hills on the sixth day. He then travelled fifteen days over hard ground, on which the camels left no trace; then three days on hard sand, and then entered the hills of drifting sand. Riley's Narrative of the Shipwreck of the brig Commerce, p. 322.

[17] The Harib of Caillié, who was not fortunate in seizing the sounds of the Arabic and Berber languages, ought probably to be Gharíb غريب. M. D'Avezac (Bulletin de la Soc. de Géog. 1834, tom. II. p. 169) proposes reading 'Arib; but since the tribe of the Gharíb is mentioned in M. Gråberg af Hemsö's list of Berber names (Journal Roy. Geog. Soc. vol. VII. p. 255) and Marmol (tom. III. fol. 9,) places a tribe named Garib in the neighbourhood of Tatta, we cannot avoid concluding that the French traveller means to speak of the same tribe as the last-named author, and that its true name is El Gharíb. But in the map drawn by M. Jomard to illustrate Caillié's journey, the position of El Harib is even more faulty than its orthography. It detracts little from Caillié's merit to say, that under all the circumstances of his journey his observations of the compass were worth but little, and his estimates of distance are not to be implicitly relied on. Nineteen miles a day for the average of forty-three days between Tomboktú and El Harib, and twenty-nine miles daily during the worst part of the journey, over deep and burning sands, are rates of travelling much too high for a loaded caravan. By the undue lengthening of the early part of the route, El Harib has been carried about fifty miles too far north, so that Tatta, instead of being north-west of it, according to the traveller's text, is made to lie to the south-west. All the other bearings described are in like manner displaced. M. D'Avezac has corrected this error of latitude, but has, at the same time, unfortunately introduced a new error of longitude, and carried all his positions too far eastward.

[18] Quart. Rev. No. 75, 1828, p. 102; Edinburgh Phil. Journal, vol. IV. p. 42.

The vast expanse of light sand thrown up into wave-like hillocks, which change with every wind, is a remarkable feature of the great desert, depending not more on the mineralogical constitution of the country than on the excessive dryness of the climate. The permanence of its general position, therefore, in spite of local fluctuations, is as certain as its extension from west to east, between the zones fertilized by rains. Now the site of Támedelt was four or five days westward from El Harib; and since on the road to Tomboktú from the former of these places the loose sand is entered on the twenty-fifth day, from the latter on the twenty-third; while from Támedelt to Aúdaghost the sands were entered also on the twenty-third day, there is reason to infer, that so far, the direction of the road from Sús el Aḳṣa to Aúdaghost differed little, if at all, from the modern road to Tomboktú. The ancient and modern roads to Negroland ran nearly parallel between the hills south of Sús el Aḳṣa and the zone of drifting sands.

The most difficult part of the journey, according to El Bekrí, lay over the ridges of loose sand, on entering which there was no water to be found till, after four days' toil, the traveller reached the wells of Wanzamín, where all the roads to Negroland met together.[19] The roads thus said to meet that from Sijilmésah must have been those from Wergelán, Twát, and Télemsén or Tremecen. Now the roads from these places to Tomboktú all unite at Telig, about thirty days from El Harib, and our hypothesis respecting the position of Aúdaghost derives no slight confirmation from the circumstance that it gives to the meeting of the roads to that place, twenty-seven days from Támedelt, a position which harmonizes perfectly with their present junction on the road to Tomboktú. Near the meeting of the roads was a mountain, the recesses of which concealed bands of various tribes of the Zenágah, as the Lamṭah, Gezúlah, Geráwah, &c., all from the south-western extremity of Atlas, who lay in wait to attack caravans.

From the wells of Wanzamín the road continued through sand-hills in the province of Wárán for five days to a large well belonging to the Benú Wáreth, thence in two days to

[19] Wanzamín ونزمين MS. B.M.; Wabermin, Not. et Extr. p. 614.

Agharef, and in three more to Akríri, that is to say, the reservoir of water.[20] Near this place was a mountain named Azgúnán, where caravans were in danger of being attacked by the Blacks.[21] One day further, over hot sands, lay the brackish wells of Wárán, then, for three days, fresh water was found in wells belonging to the Zenágah, and another day led over the high mountain, at the foot of which stood Aúdaghost. This town was situate in a hilly country, within the limits of the rains, and does not appear to have had any water but that of wells. It can hardly be supposed that the limit of the rains in the interior of the African continent, at a distance from the sea coast, ascends beyond the twentieth parallel of latitude.[22] Now if a distance of forty days' journey be measured from Támedelt, so as to intersect the twentieth parallel towards the interior, it will be found that fifteen days' journey south-westward (according to the distance and bearing of Aúkar from Aúdaghost) measured from that intersection, will reach to the neighbourhood of Tomboktú.

The foregoing account is evidently that of a route frequented by caravans, and therefore the distances mentioned in it may

---

[20] Wárán وَارَان. The name of the inhabitants of this part of the desert has been read by M. Quatremère, Benú Hareth, instead of Benú Wareth وارث; but the restoration of this name is important; since we learn from another passage in El Bekrí that the Benú Wareth were to the east of the Lumtúnah; and are thus enabled to perceive that the road to Aúdaghost lay eastwards from the road to Ghánah.—Agharef أَغْوَف MS. B.M. 102 v.—Akríri أقوري Not. et Extr. p. 615. أقرسدى MS. B.M.

[21] Azjúnán (pronounced Azgúnán) ازجونان MS. B.M.; Arkounat, Not. et Extr.

[22] In Nubia showers of rain are of rare occurrence north of the 18th parallel (Rüppell, Reisen in Nubien, &c. p. 75). Denham (Travels, &c. I. p. 164) fixed the first appearance of fresh vegetation and the limit of the tropical rains on his route to Bornú, near the 16th parallel, which is probably too low for the limit of rain. Tomboktú, we are told, has annually six weeks or more of rain (Proc. Afr. Assoc. I. p. 285; Narrative of R. Adams, p. 42)—and this blessing seems to extend some distance north-eastward of it (Riley's Narrative, p. 346). Towards the coast the gum forests which extend as far north as the 18th degree of latitude probably do not fall far short of the limit of regular rains.

be received with confidence. Its general direction, as Abulfedá tells us, was to the south. El Bekrí describes also the journey from Daràh to Ghánah, in a brief and uncircumstantial manner; but his description, though wanting in the minuteness and precision derivable from the experience of caravans, is yet not wholly uninstructive. From Wádi Daràh to Wádi Tárḳa, on the margin of the desert, was a journey of five days. Then the traveller entered the wilderness in which water occurred only every two or three days. Of the wells first met with, one was called Tezámt. Eastward of it were Bír el Ḥammálín, or the porters' well, and another named Nálellí or Málekí.[23] "From these wells," says our author, "to the country of Islám, is a distance of four days; and at an equal distance are the Adarérén Wazzél, or mountains of iron.[24] There a desert begins in which there is no water for eight days; it is, indeed, that which is emphatically styled The Desert. The water in it belongs to the Benú Yentesír, a tribe of Zenágah. The village of Moddúken, which is next arrived at, belongs to the same race. Thence to Ghánah is a journey of four days."[25]

---

[23] Tarḳá ترقا Not. et Extr. p. 623; Tárga تارجي MS. B.M. 105 r.—Tezámt تزامت MS. B.M. 105 v; Baramet, Not. et Extr. p. 624.—Bir el Ḥammálín بير الحمالين—Máleki مالكي Not. et Extr. p. 264; Nálelliناللي MS. B.M. 105 v.

[24] In the Parisian MS. the expression is "the mountains, the name of which, in Berber, signifies *the mountains of iron.*" Not. et Extr. 624. But the MS. B.M. gives the Berber name Adarérén wazzél أدَرارَن وزّال in which Adarérén is the plural of Adrar, a mountain, and wazzél, iron, corresponds with the *ouzail* of Shaw's vocabulary (Travels in Barbary, II. p. 382).

[25] Yentesír ينتسير, MS. B.M.; Belis, Not. et Extr.—Moddúken مدّوكن MS. B.M.; Merouken, Not. et Extr. From the village of Moddúken, which belonged to the Zenágah, to the city of Ghánah مدينة غانة was a journey of only four days. But for Ghánah in this place M. Quatremère proposes reading Akka, عاقة, being perplexed by the faultiness of his MS. which seems to conduct beyond Ghánah to the country of the Lumtúnah. The MS. B.M. p. 105 v, clears up the

Wádi Darȧh was three days from Támedelt, probably east by north. Wádi Tárḳa may be conjectured to have been on the southern side of the mountains of Azawwar mentioned in the account of the route to Aúdaghost. But the particular here chiefly deserving of attention, is The Desert, in which no water was met with for eight days. The name of this desert, omitted by El Bekrí, is supplied by subsequent writers. We are informed that the merchants going to Ghánah passed through the desert of Tíser, a dry and desolate wilderness of sand, with only a few pools of bad water, the chief of which was that called the well of Tíser.[26] The extent of this desert is variously stated to be eight, ten, twelve, and even fourteen days' journey.[27] At its eastern extremity stood Aúdaghost, and hence it is not surprising that the journey to that city should present diminished difficulty; though the loose, hot sands, and intervals of four or five days without water, in the latter half of the route thither, between the 23rd and 32nd days, clearly mark the continuation of the inhospitable tract.[28]

---

difficulty by these words; "and from the wells before mentioned, (viz. the wells of El Ḥammálín and Nálelli,) the water is carried a four days' journey to Mount Aízal or Izal إيزل in the desert," &c. Thus the road to the desert (the Lumtúnah not being named in this passage) does not begin from Ghánah, but from "the before-mentioned wells." Jebel Aízal may be suspected of being another form of Adarérén Wazzél.

[26] The name Tíser تيسر (Jaubert's Idrísí. Recueil de Mém. &c. tom. v. p. 106) is extremely doubtful. Some of the MS. copies of Idrísí have Níser نيسر, others Nesír نسير. The epitome offers Bansar بنسر; Abulfedá writes Yasr يسر.

[27] El Bekrí (Not. et Extr. 624) gives to the absolutely waterless desert between Sijilmésah and Ghánah, an extent of eight days' journey. Sherı́shí, in his commentary on Harírí (Moallakah 9) gives it a width of ten days. Ibn el Wardi increases it to twelve days, and El Idrísí (Jaubert's Transl. p. 106) to fourteen. It was natural enough that the first of these writers, who may be supposed to have derived much of his information from the early Morabites themselves, should receive a less exaggerated account of the inhospitable nature of the western desert than those who followed him.

[28] The road to Aúdaghost passed through the territory of the Benú Wáreth. But this tribe were to the east of the Lumtúnah, through whose country was traced the

On the west, the desert of Tíser adjoined the division of the Ṣaḥrá called Kamnúdíyah, which bordered on the ocean in the vicinity of Cape Bojador, as shall be shown hereafter. Unless we assign, therefore, to the territorial divisions of the Ṣaḥrá a disproportionate extension from west to east, the contiguity of the maritime district of Kamnúdíyah to the desert of Tíser, strengthens the presumption that the latter could hardly have reached beyond the twelfth meridian from the shores of the Atlantic; or, in other words, that it did not extend far east of the meridian of Tomboktú, and, consequently, that the road to this city from the north passes over the tract of desert anciently named Tíser.

But it will naturally be asked, is there such a tract of peculiarly arid desert on the road to Tomboktú? Certainly there is; a desert of like extent, presenting the same physical character, and occupying a similar position in the route. Ibn Baṭúṭah, on his way from Sijilmésah to Tomboktú, arrived at Tegháza, near the edge of the desert, in twenty-five days. In ten days more, he came to the wells, or rather muddy pools of Táserahlá, where the caravan halted to prepare for the march over the formidable waste of sand, which it required ten days to traverse in order to reach Aïwalátin, a town on the southern border of the Ṣaḥrá.[29] Had that traveller crossed

---

road to Ghánah (see note 20). And Ghánah was at least four days south of the desert of Tíser, while Aúdaghost was east of that desert, according to Abulfedá (Büsching's Magazin, vol. IV. p. 212). El Idrísí also places Aúdaghost in the northern part of the kingdom of Ghánah; and by stating its distance from Wergelán and Jermah, he plainly intimates that it was likewise in the eastern part. All these particulars combine to prove that Aúdaghost was to the north-east of Ghánah.

[29] Ibn Baṭuṭah travelled at the slow rate of a heavily laden caravan. Halts included, he was two months in reaching Aïwalátin, or Walata, on the southern border of the desert. His accounts of the pools of Táserahlá which shall be given hereafter, exactly correspond with El Idrísí's description of the wells of Tíser. In Jaubert's 'Idrísí' (p. 11), is the following passage: "Il y existe cependant des mares d'eau de pluie qu'on rencontre après deux, quatre, cinq ou douze journées de marche, semblables à celle du désert situé sur la route de Sedjelmasa à Ghana, et où l'on ne trouve de l'eau qu'au bout de quatorze jours de marche." Instead of the word *desert* in this place, the Epitome of El Idrísí has the name Bansar بنسر, evidently for Tíser تيسر.

obliquely from Táserahlá to Tomboktú, he might perhaps have found the waterless desert to exceed a ten days' journey in extent. But towards the east its width seems to diminish; whether it be that the northward course of the Great River, or the chain of mountains determining that circuit of the stream, and stretching across into the desert, modifies the atmosphere so as to give a greater range to the periodic rains in that meridian, we have no means of deciding. But the whole of the western Ṣaḥrá and the peculiar tract under consideration, are described by Leo Africanus in the following manner:—

"To begin with the desert of Zenaga; this is a dry and barren tract beginning from the ocean on the west, and extending eastward to the salt pits of Tegaza. On the north it is bounded by Numidia; that is to say, by Sus, Acca, and Darah; and it extends towards the south as far as the land of the Blacks; that is to say, to the kingdom of Gualata and Tombutto. There is no water found in it, except at intervals of a hundred miles, and this, after all, is salt and bitter, in wells of great depth, particularly on the road from Segelmesse to Tombutto. There are many wild animals and serpents in it, as shall be related in the proper place. In this waste is found a desert very difficult and dismal, called Azaoad, where neither water nor dwelling-place is met with for two hundred miles, from the well of Azaoad to the well of Araoan, which is a hundred and fifty miles from Tombutto, and in which great numbers of men and animals perish of heat and thirst." [30]

[30] Leo Afr. pt. VI. c. 54. Marmol writes Azaoat. Beyond, or eastward of the desert of the Zenágah, Leo places that of the Zuenziga, "which extends from Segelmesse, Tebelbelt, and Benigorai, to the desert of Ghir, in the south, which faces the kingdom of Gubar. On the west it has Tegaza, and on the east the desert of Air, inhabited by the Targa tribe (the Tawárik)." It is manifest that the several divisions of the desert described by Leo (pt. VI. c. 54—8), all extend from north-west to south-east, conformably to the boundary line which we have ascribed to the country of the Zenágah on the east. It is plain also, that these people were not in the vicinity of the Houssa country. The desert of Ghir brings to mind the Káhir كاهر of Ibn Baṭuṭah; but we can have no doubt that the Air of Leo is the country of Ahír (Ḥáj Ḳásim in Walckenaer, Rech. p. 448) or Aáheer ('Ahír?), which we learn from Sultan Bello (Denham's Travels, II. 447, where Aáheer is erroneously

The same writer elsewhere informs us, that the desert of Azawad was so called from its barrenness and dryness. It is not unreasonable to suppose that when the local designation of Tíser fell into disuse, the epithet expressing the general aspect of the region took its place. The name Azawad still remains to the tract of desert northward of Tomboktú.[31] And it cannot escape attention that the deserts of Tíser and Azawad resemble each other not only in extent and physical character, but that they are also equidistant from Sijilmésah; that they are both on the road southward from it, and both reaching to the southern limit of the Ṣaḥrá. There is still another point of resemblance between them, which, of itself, is almost sufficient to prove their common identity. El Bekrí remarks, that in travelling from Sijilmésah to Ghánah, a desert of two months' journey was traversed, in which there were no fixed habitations, and the only people met with were wanderers, such as the Benú Masúfah, a branch of the Zenágah. The Benú Masúfah then, were in the middle of the eleventh century the tenants of the inhospitable plains over which lay the road to Ghánah; and it is remarkable that, three centuries later, the same miserable tribe hovered over the road to Tomboktú. Ibn Baṭúṭah found them to be the regular, and, as it were, hereditary guides across that desert, with the intricacies of

---

said to be south of Bornú) to be the portion of the desert lying north of Houssa and Bornú. But it appears that the name in question has extended further southwards since Leo's time, a proof that the Tawárik have been gaining ground.

[31] The account of Major Laing's journey to Tomboktú (Quarterly Review, July 1828, p. 103–5), after stating that he was attacked by the Tawárik, makes frequent mention of *Azoad*, whence, on recovering from his wounds, he wrote his last letter. Caillié mentions "the tribe of Zaouât, who wander in the desert of *the same name*" (Voyage à Temboctou, tom. II. p. 349). It was the Sheikh of this tribe, Hamet aúlád Habíb, who put Major Laing to death, meeting him five days north of Tomboktú, on the road to Arawan. The name of this murderer brings to mind the fact that the chief wells on the roads to Aúdaghost and Ghánah were dug by a Sheikh of the Aúlád Habíb. It is plain that the tribe called Zaouât by Caillié, were so named from their country; and it is probable that he, or the editor of his volumes, deprived the name Azawad of its initial letter, in the belief that it was thereby freed from the Arabic article. The desert of Azawad is described by Lyon (Trav. in N. Afr. p. 148) under the name of 'Asheríyah, or *the ten days'* desert.

which, tradition as well as personal experience had made them perfectly acquainted. In a region where the natural landmarks are so broad and unchangeable, and where man is comparatively so weak; where there is so little to tempt ambition or to nourish caprice, and where the whole tribe laying claim to a long extent of territory, could never exceed a handful of individuals,—the fact that the roads to Ghánah and Tomboktú, traced over peculiarly arid and forbidding tracts, both passed through the encampments of the same tribe, is a strong proof of the proximity of those roads: for the occupiers of the most inhospitable region in which life can with difficulty be supported, are not likely to be disturbed in their possessions.

It has been seen that Leo Africanus represents the country of the Zenágah, or Ṣinhájah, to have extended from the sea shore as far eastward as Tegháza and Tomboktú. He obviously meant to intimate that the road to Tomboktú formed the eastern boundary of that nation or division of the Berbers. But his expressions are not such as require to be strictly interpreted; on the contrary, they have a claim to that latitude of explanation which reconciles them with the state of things at present, when the Zenágah occupy the country round Tomboktú and to a short distance eastward of it. His expressions, however, militate most strongly against any hypothesis which would place Aúdaghost remote from Tomboktú, since the road to the former of those cities lay wholly within the limits of the Zenágah. If these people held as large a share of the Ṣaḥrá in the beginning of the sixteenth century as in the middle of the eleventh,—and, since they figured as conquerors in the only revolution generally affecting them in the meantime, this can hardly be disputed,—it must follow that the road to Aúdaghost, being within their limits, could not have passed far eastward of Tomboktú.

The Zenágah extended southward, according to Leo, "to the country of the Blacks, where are the kingdoms of Gualata and Tombutto." To the words, "the country of the Blacks," Marmol, while borrowing largely from the Arab writer, adds the gloss, "which is called Geneúa." [32] And herein he accords

---

[32] Marmol, Descripcion de Africa, vol. I. fol. 34 r. In another place, however,

with all other authorities respecting the position of Genéwah, which region, however vaguely defined, is yet always placed on the frontiers of Negroland, westward from Tomboktú. In early ages however, before the Berbers had derived strength from Arab instruction, the Blacks probably possessed a larger share of the desert, or at least the name Genéwah reached further northward. An Arab writer informs us, that Genéwah extended from the ocean in the west, to the country of Wergelán in the east, and from Amímah in the south to Arkí and Núl el Akṣa in the north.[33] The longitudinal dimensions of this country are here expressed in terms of obvious inaccuracy. Wergelán, though far to the north-east of the country called Genéwah, is yet made conterminous with it, owing to the great share which that Berber state took in the commerce of Negroland, at that time concentred in Ghánah. But the line on which the breadth of Genéwah is measured, drawn from north to south, from Arkí to Amímah, may be presumed to mark its central or principal section. Now Arkí was on the hills of the Lumtúnah, seven days distant from Wád Nún, and Amímah stood at a short distance westward or south-westward from the future site of Tomboktú.[34] The mean position of

---

(vol. III. fol. 16,) he uses the name Genéwah in a restricted sense, and says that the Zenágah have on the south, "the Benais, Gelofes, the kingdoms of Gualata, Geneúa, Meli, and Tumbuto"—Genéwah being here evidently identified, by hypothesis, with Jenni.

[33] Kitábu-l-Járáfíyah (Book of Geography), &c. MS. in the collection of D. P. de Gayangos. This anonymous work, though ill written, contains much which is not to be found in El Idrísí and his numerous copiers.

[34] Arkí أَرِكي MS. B.M. fol. 107 ; Azdji أَرجي Not. et Extr. p. 629.—The copies of El Idrísí present this name in a variety of forms. In M. Jaubert's translation of this author (p. 206), there is the following passage: "La ville s'appelle Azoucaï ازقي en langue Berbère, et Cocadam قوقدم en génois." By *génois* we are here to understand the language of the Genéwah. But the name here read Cocadam, or, as we should write it, Ḳúḳdem, deserves a moment's notice. Leo Africanus informs us (pt. VI. c. 55) that the caravans from Telemsén to Tomboktú, pass over a difficult tract of desert, where no water is found for nine days, and which is named Gogdem. It is probable that this desert, as well as the town further west,

Genéwah being thus indicated, the author adds, "and of its cities, is Ghánah."[35] Here, then, is another proof that Ghánah was contiguous to the western desert and to western Negroland, and that the tract of country in which it stood and flourished, was the same in which Tomboktú subsequently rose into importance.

The country assigned to Genéwah, in the above-cited passage, really belonged for the most part to the Zenágah, who, anterior to their conversion to Mohammedanism, lived much intermin-

---

owed its name to wanderers from Goghidem, a mountain of central Atlas, in the province of Hascora, of whose emigration Leo himself furnishes the explanation (pt. II. c. 71). Arkí, the chief town of the Lumtúnah, is placed by El Idrísí, seven days from Wád Nún. As little reliance, however, can be placed on that author's measures, we may allow Arkí to be even fourteen days from Wád Nún, and yet its site will not be eastward of the road to Tomboktú. But, according to El Idrísí (*ut supra*), those who went to Silla, Tekrúr, and Ghánah, passed near it of necessity. Our knowledge of the position of Mímah, or Amímah, we owe to Ibn Baṭúṭah, whose narrative shall be examined further on.

[35] Ghánah, in the country of Genéwah, من بلاد جناوة is an expression frequently used by the same author. Where others would have written Beléd es-Súdán, or land of the Blacks, he always writes Genéwah. This name, indeed, became in Morocco the general designation of blacks and slaves. Thus we are told that Muley Hamed grew rich "by husbanding his Maseraws (oil-mills) and Ingenewas (slave farms) where his sugar canes did grow. (A True Historical Discovery of Muley Hamet's Rising, &c. 1609, c. 3.) The initial letter of the name Genéwah جناوة being pronounced hard by the Moors, the southern Europeans, in imitation of them, wrote Chinoia, Gheneoa, and Ghinéa; from which we, by throwing back the accent, made Guinea. "The kingdom, says Leo (pt. VI. c. 3), called by our merchants (the Moors) Gheneoa, is by the natives called Genni, and by the Europeans who have any knowledge of it, Ghinea." It is certain that Ghinéa and Guinea are derived from Genéwah; but we see no sufficient reason to admit that the name of the city of Genni or Jenni has the same origin. But since general names, not merely appellations, are rare among a rude people, it is natural for us to inquire what was meant by Genéwah, or, to conform to the sound, Ghinéwah. Did it mean *the Blacks?* On the coast, the negroes contiguous to the Whites are, for contradistinction, named in their own language Wolof, that is, *Blacks*. The name Jelofe (Wolof) is used in this general sense by Marmol (III. fol. 27 v). And why should not the people of the interior designate themselves according to the same universal and simple principle? Now, in the language of Tomboktú, *gnewa*, or, as Major Rennell, who had the original information, writes it, *genewa*, signifies Black (Proc.

gled with the Blacks. The latter may have had the upper hand; or, though in a servile state, they may have been the more numerous class of the inhabitants; or finally, the slave trade being carried on universally in the desert, the Arabs of Barbary may have easily confounded the country exporting slaves with that which produced them; and thus applied the name Genéwah to the deserts of which Berber tribes were, if not the sole occupants, at least the masters. But the movements of the Morabites revealed more completely the partition and social condition of the Ṣaḥrá. The northern portion of it, towards the ocean, was possessed by the Lumtúnah, whose dwellings covered a range of hills (probably those called by El Bekrí Azawwar) said to be six days' journey in length, and to be shaded by 20,000 palm trees.[36] On these hills, and about seven days from Wád Nún, stood the fort or town of Arkí, the chief place of the Lumtúnah, whose flocks wandered from the shores of the ocean as far eastward as the road to Ghánah.

South of the Lumtúnah, but separated from them by an uninhabited tract ten days' journey in width, were the Benú Goddálah, the most powerful of the Berber tribes. In the uninhabited tract ten days wide, it is easy to recognize the sandy region south of Cape Bojador, and forming the continuation of the desert of Tíser or Azawad. The country of the Benú Goddálah is said to have extended a two months' journey in length and breadth, a description which is applied also to the whole western Ṣaḥrá, and to the dominions of Ghánah; and considering that in each case the Atlantic Ocean is taken as a boundary, it is evident enough that no exact limits were set to territorial possessions in the desert, and that claims of sovereignty often extended from opposite quarters over the same ground.[37]

Afr. Ass. I. p. 124 and 428), so that we are justified in suspecting at least that we have here found the origin of the name Genéwah.

36 Not. et Extr. p. 629.

37 The extent of desert here assigned to the Benú Goddálah, may enable us, if carefully considered, to ascertain their interior limits towards Ghánah. Numerous authorities, which need not be here cited, agree in estimating the distance of Tomboktú from Táfílélt or Morocco to be, in general terms, a two months' journey.

In the country of the Benú Goddálah was a mine or natural deposit of salt near a town or place of fixed habitation on the sea shore, called Aúlíl. At this place was a point of land, or peninsula, insulated by the tide, but accessible on foot at low

---

The more circumstantial accounts reckon, between Tomboktú and Akka, Tatta, or El Harib, near the frontiers of Sús and the desert, thirty-six (Jackson's Morocco, p. 241)—forty-three (Shabeeny's Narrative, by Jackson, p. 7)—or thirty-nine days (Caillié, Journal, &c.), exclusive of halts. We find the distance of Tatta from Tomboktú estimated also at fifty days (Proceedings of the African Association, vol. I. p. 225). Davidson (Notes on a Journey in Africa, 1839, p. 101) learned that the courier's track from Wád Nún to Tomboktú is travelled in forty days, and that from the same place to Jenni is usually reckoned a distance of sixty days, though frequently traversed in less time (Notes, &c. p. 113). But it must be observed, that, with respect to caravans, the time allowed for halting at the chief wells often exceeds that spent in travelling. Now to estimate the longitudinal dimensions of the western desert, we have the distance of forty days' journey from Arguin to the French factory at Fort St. Joseph, on the Senegal, and from the latter point forty-eight days to Tomboktú, the latter distance being established by a concurrence of testimony which places it beyond dispute (D'Anville, Mem. de l'Acad. tom. XXVI. p. 73; Rennell in Proc. of Afr. Assoc. vol. II. pp. 225, 464). Circuits being allowed for, these distances combined will place Tomboktú about two months and a half from Arguin. In confirmation of this conclusion, we find that Sidi Hamet (Riley's Narrative, p. 319), taking the road by the sea shore, travelled from Wád Nún southwards for four months to the borders of Negroland, and then went eastward two months to Tomboktú. On his return he travelled westward one month, and encamped at a little Negro town called Jathrow—probably the Dgazzara of M. Roger's informant (Rec. de Voy. II. p. 62), whose estimate of distances, however, uniformly fall far short of the reality. Sidi Hamet then turned northward, and reached Wád Nún in three months and a half. Though the people dwelling on the margin of the desert are apt to talk of speedy journeys, as was experienced by Park and Davidson, yet the inhabitants of the wilderness itself, having little provision and weak cattle, which they pasture as they go, rarely travel at a rate exceeding twelve or thirteen miles a day. Alexander Scott (Edinburgh Phil. Jour. vol. IV.), a shipwrecked sailor, and captive in the desert, travelled from the vicinity of Cape Bojador two months and a half, to the line of gum forests, which lie chiefly between the 17th and 18th parallels, and then continued his march for another month before he reached Lake Dibbie, which is formed by the waters of the Great River. It is needless to collect more authorities to show that a desert of two months in extent and bounded by the Atlantic, must be supposed to lie wholly westward of Tomboktú.

water. Close to it was the port. Ambergris was collected on it at the sea side, and turtle, which constituted the chief food of the inhabitants, were there so large, that fishermen, as our author assevers, went to sea in their shells. From Aúlíl salt was carried inland to Ghánah and other cities of the Blacks. The road from the same place to Wád Nún was a two months' journey in length, going along the sea shore, where fresh water was found by digging in the sand when the tide was out.[38]

There is little room for doubt or hesitation in determining the position of Aúlíl. One point only on the whole coast of the Ṣaḥrá can be selected for it with any show of reason: and that point is in the bay of Arguin, where the natural deposits of salt, the little island or peninsula, and the abundance of large tortoises, are all found together; and exactly at a distance of two months' journey from Wád Nún, along the shore.[39] At Arguin also existed, in the fifteenth century, a trade derived from the natural productions of the place, exactly similar to that ascribed to Aúlíl in the eleventh century. Since the shores of the Great Desert offer one locality, and but one, answering to the description given by El Bekrí of Aúlíl, we must necessarily conclude that this town was situate in that locality,—namely, near Cape St. Anne in the bay of Arguin.[40]

---

[38] Aúlíl اوليل. It is also written Aúlílí اوليلي by Ibn el Wardi and others. It is probably a variation of the name Walílí وليلي, formerly belonging to a village near Fez, and also to Tangier.

[39] If the well-ascertained route of forty-eight days from Fort St. Joseph to Tomboktú, measured on Mr. J. Arrowsmith's map, be taken as the scale, and sixty days be then measured along the shore from Wád Nún, it will exactly reach Arguin. But the Benú Goddálah, possessing a desert of two months in extent, were separated by a six days' journey from the Ṣínghánah, who dwelt on the river between Silla and Ghánah. Now from Arguin to the nearest point of the Great River, towards the east, is a distance of about sixty-eight days' journey, measured as above. It is necessary, therefore, if we would treat El Bekrí as a sensible and sober writer, to infer that Aúlíl was at Arguin, and that the Ṣínghánah dwelt near Lake Debú, between Silla and Tomboktú.

[40] At Cape St. Anne, in the bay of Arguin, where the beds of salt are found, is a small island which appears to answer El Bekrí's description. Labat (L'Afrique Occidentale, tom. I. p. 58) says of it, "On trouve à la pointe de la Saline une petite isle qui ne se distingue presque pas du continent." De Barros (Decad. I.

Thus it appears that the Benú Goddálah were the possessors of the maritime region of the Ṣaḥrá, from Cape Blanco southwards. They also extended far inland (a two months' journey, as has been already stated), and were separated by a distance of only six days from the Blacks on the Great River, and in the vicinity of Ghánah. They were the possessors, therefore, of the vast country which is now divided among the Ludayas, Brebísh, Trarzas, Erghebat, and others. Though esteemed the most powerful of the Berber tribes, they were yet compelled to yield the pre-eminence to the Lumtúnah, in the wars which immediately preceded the coalition of both under the name of Morabites. It may be fairly assumed, therefore, that these great tribes which divided between them the entire breadth of the Ṣaḥrá where it was least inhospitable, constituted the main body of the Berber nation to which they belonged; and therefore that the road to Aúdaghost, which left them on the west, lay near to the limit of the country occupied by the Zenágah, and consequently passed through the same tract as the road subsequently traced to Tomboktú.

Having thus examined the routes from Sijilmésah to Ghánah, and briefly surveyed the state of the western deserts, with a view to illustrate the geographical position of the latter country, we may now proceed to consider also its internal condition and character; to inquire who were its neighbours in Negroland; how these were placed in relation to each other; and how far the accounts given of them, taken collectively and in the plainest acceptation, accord with the knowledge which we at present possess of the interior of Africa.

Aúdaghost, once the residence, as we are told, of the king styled Ghánah, was situate in a hilly country, on the margin of the desert, but within the limit of the summer rains. Its water was chiefly drawn from wells; its irrigated gardens had small extent, yet to eyes accustomed only to the monotony of the sandy waste, the groups of palm trees around it formed a luxuriant scene. Its population, gathered from various tribes in the Belédu-l-Jeríd, belonged chiefly to the

---

liv. I. c. 10) explains why Arguin is the only inhabited spot on the shores of the Desert.

Berber nation of the Zenátah.[41] Nor is it difficult to explain why an isolated Zenátah population should fix and maintain itself in immediate contact with the roving and predatory Zenágah; for during the period referred to in these accounts, Sijilmésah, with which Aúdaghost was connected by ties of commerce, belonged to the Zenátah. The latter town was, in reality, but a trading colony on the frontiers of Negroland; and its mercantile inhabitants, content with the town and trade, seem to have never affected political independence.

In the year of the Hijra 350 (A.D. 961), the king of Aúdaghost was Tín Yerátán, son of Wasenbú, of the Zenágah nation. His empire is said to have had an extent of two months' journey in length and breadth, and more than twenty negro kings paid tribute to him. But, at a later period, Aúdaghost became tributary to Ghánah. This submission of a Berber people to a nation of Blacks and unbelievers, served as a pretext to the Morabites, who, in 446, (A.D. 1054, the same year in which they made themselves masters of Sijilmésah,) destroyed Aúdaghost, carrying off the women and children into slavery.[42] Arab writers, of a later date than the fifth century of the Hijra, still speak of Aúdaghost and its Zenágah rulers. It is not unlikely that, regardless of events, they only re-echo the words of ancient historians; otherwise, we must snppose that place to have revived for a short time under the descendants of its Morabite conquerors. But the same revolution which yielded up the old and circuitous channel of commerce to the owners of the Western Desert, must have tended to let it fall into disuse. Under the new state of things, the Lumtúnah and Masúfah would naturally take the nearest road to Ghánah, through their own country and over the desert of Tíser; and thus Aúdaghost would be forgotten.[43]

---

[41] El Bekrí in Not. et Extr. p. 630. It is Abulfedá, who, quoting Ibnu Sáïd, informs us (Büsching's Mag. IV. 205,) that Aúdaghost was within the limit of the rains.

[42] Not. et Extr. p. 631. The fact that the campaign of the Morabites in one year embraced both Aúdaghost and Sijilmésah, is enough to show that the former place was contiguous to the Western Ṣaḥrá.

[43] The language of El Idrísí (Rec. de Voy. v. p. 109), paints the decay of

The trade centering in Aúdaghost embraced not only the gold and slaves of Negroland, but also the productions of the Western Desert, and of the shores of the Atlantic Ocean. The skins of the antelope called Dant, or Lant, were wrought into bucklers by its artisans; who also manufactured ambergris, their supplies of which, we are told, they owed to their vicinity to the sea shore.[44] From this it may be concluded, not that Aúdaghost was near the sea, but that, in those early times, the possessors of the Western Ṣaḥrá were generally in too wild a state to allow trade to be carried on through their country; and that consequently the maritime productions of Aúlíl passed eastwards through the hands of the Benú Goddálah (who, occupying a favoured tract, had acquired more settled habits) to Aúdaghost, and thus reached Sijilmésah, after making the circuit of the domains of the rude Zenágah. El Bekrí says also, that on the hills round Aúdaghost grew trees yielding the gum which was used in Spain to dress silks.[45] Though this statement is not improbable, yet it is more likely that the Benú Goddálah, while conveying their salt and amber to the interior, likewise carried thither the produce of their rich gum forests. Wealth in Aúdaghost consisted chiefly in slaves, of which single individuals sometimes possessed a thousand each. That mercantile spirit had there fixed its abode in the midst of natural sterility, is forcibly expressed in the acknowledgment that slaves were the only luxury of the place. Aúdaghost

---

Aúdaghost: he describes it to be "a little town, deficient in water; with a scanty population and miserable trade, which consists in camels." This is the town which modern geographers, induced by a supposed resemblance of names—though Rennell (Geogr. Illust. of Park's Journey, in Proc. of Afr. Assoc. I. p. 501,) took the precaution to convert Aúdaghost into Agadost—have chosen to identify with Aghades, or Aghdes, which Leo Africanus (pt. VII. c. 9), writing in 1541, calls "a city built by the moderns;" while Marmol (III. fol. 24), more precise, says that it was founded 160 years before the time of his writing, or in 1438.

44 Not. et Extr. p. 630. Bucklers made of the skins of the Dant or Lant (probably el-ant), which is supposed to be the *Antilope Leucorix*, were chiefly manufactured in Wád Nún. By the amber carried to Aúdaghost from the sea shore, we must understand ambergris, to which El Idrísí alludes when describing the western shores of Africa (Rec. de Voy. pp. 64 and 135).

45 Not. et Extr. p. 615.

exhibited the extreme licentiousness of manners characteristic, as will appear from other examples occurring in these pages, of all the towns in the southern border of the great desert, where the traveller, just escaped from the perils of the wilderness, indulges in the pleasures offered by a degraded population; and where the recklessness usual in a seaport is increased by the opportunities of the slave-mart.

After the destruction of Aúdaghost by the Morabites, Aúkár, fifteen days distant from it towards the south-west, became the capital of Ghánah; or rather that capital was composed of two towns, viz.—Aúkár, inhabited by Mohammedans, and containing no less than twelve mosques; and Ghábah, where the king resided, in the midst of a black population.[46] Dark woods environed the latter town, and spread a gloom well suited to the pagan rites for the performance of which they were reserved, and which often involved the sacrifice of human victims. An interval of six miles, covered with habitations, separated the two towns. The inhabitants drew their water from wells. The climate was deadly to all but the natives.

El Bekrí's description of Ghánah evidently brings us within the limits of Negroland. It exhibits to us, on the one hand, the Blacks summoned before their king by beat of drum, sprinkling dust on their heads, and prostrating themselves in his presence; or performing the rites of their cruel superstitions in the darkness of their woods: and, on the other, the Arabs or Berbers dwelling apart in a more elevated and open situation, and yet suffering from the noxious humidity of the air. But, it is to be remarked, that he makes no mention of running waters, the importance of which no Arab author ever overlooks; and indeed, it must be inferred from that author's words, that there was no river—certainly no great river—in the immediate vicinity of the capital of Ghánah.

---

[46] Ghábah غابة MS. B.M. fol. 112 r; Alghábat الغابت Rec. de Voy. II. p. 2; Ghaïah غاية Not. et Extr. 643. The predominant idea in the meaning of the name Ghábah or Ghábaṯ, which is undoubtedly the true reading, is ***obscurity:*** lowness of situation and overhanging gloom are both implied by it.

The Benú Goddálah, who possessed the southern portion of the Ṣaḥrá from the shores of the ocean eastwards, carried their salt and other merchandise to the Ṣínghánah, the nearest black nation, from whom they were separated by a distance of only six days' journey, and whose chief city stood on both banks of the Great River, called the Nile of the Blacks. When it is considered that the Lumtúnah reached within ten days of Ghánah; that they were separated from the Goddálah by a broad tract of uninhabitable sand; and that all accounts agree in representing Ghánah as the most western of the kingdoms of the Blacks,—or, in other words, that the desert alone intervened between it and the ocean; it will be apparent that the Ṣínghánah, who were nearest to the Goddálah, lay towards the south or south-west from Ghánah.[47] South-westward from the Ṣínghánah, at no great distance, was Tekrúr, and a little further on stood Silla, both likewise on the Great River or Nile of the Blacks. The last-named place was twenty days' journey from Ghánah; and, from what has been already said, it will be manifest that its bearing from that capital was between south and south-west.[48]

---

[47] Ṣínghánah صينغانة. Caillié (tom. II. p. 237) mentions a place called Sangouno, on the left bank of the Great River, three or four days from Jenni.—Tekrúr تكرور.

[48] Silla سلي, سيلي, and سلا. El Bekrí mentions cotton as one of the chief productions of this country; no house, he says, was without its cotton tree. Leo, in like manner, says (pt. VII. c. 3), that cotton was the staple merchandise of Jenni, which is but two days from Silla; and Caillié observed the general cultivation of that article in the country south-westward of Jenni (tom. II. pp. 156–167.) The people of Silla, being slave-dealers, made constant war on their pagan neighbours, of whom the nearest were the Kalembú قلنبو, a day's journey distant. Now the district of Negroland at present characterized by the termination *bú*, is that contiguous to the modern Silla towards the west, and on the northern side of the river. There we find Modiboo, Doolinkeaboo, Fanimboo, &c., within a small compass. "From Tarankaṭi ترنقة (MS. B.M. fol. 111 r), near Silla, the inhabited country (says our author) extends to Záfḳú زافقو;" which name M. Quatremère reads Afnou (Not. et Extr. p. 641). But if we suppose that a Nún ن is here mistaken for the Maghrebí Kaf ڧ, the two readings will be reconciled in Zafnú, the Jafnoo of our

Going eastward from Ghánah, through Aúghám, a fertile and well-cultivated district, the traveller arrived in five days at Rás el má, or the Water-head, "where the Nile issued from the land of the Blacks." On the northern bank of the river dwelt the Merásah, a Zenágah tribe. Pagan blacks inhabited the opposite side. Six days further down the river stood Tírḳa, a market frequented by the people of Ghánah as well as of Tádmekkah. From Tírḳa the Nile turned southwards, and in three days entered the territory of the Seghmárah, a tribe depending on Tádmekkah. "On the side of the river opposite to them," observes our author, "is Kaúkaú, which belongs to the Blacks." [49]

Tádmekkah was a town situate, like Aúdaghost, on the southern frontier of the Great Desert. According to El Bekrí, it was fifty days eastward from Ghánah, fifty from Wérgelán, and forty from Ghodémis.[50] Another author, whose measures of distance are not so easily appreciated, places Tádmekkah forty days westwards from Tajúah (in the northern part of Darfur), through the country of the Molaththemún—that is, the people who muffle up or conceal their faces (the Tawárik), and thirty days eastwards from Ghánah, beyond which is the ocean.[51] These intimations combined will place

---

maps, which is a very likely limit to our author's exact information. To point out unequivocally the direction in which his narrative led him, he adds, that "the country continues populous to the ocean."

[49] Aúghám اوغام MS. B.M. 1140; Audagam اودعام Not. et Extr. p. 651—Merásah مراسة—Tírḳa تيرقي MS. B.M.—Tádmekkah تادمكة—Seghmárah سغمارة—Kaúkaú كوكو.

[50] Not. et Extr. pp. 652, 653. The ten journeys allowed between Wérgelán وارجلان MS. B.M., وارقلان Not. et Extr., and Ghodémis غدامس, show the scale by which we are to measure this route, and allow us to stretch the forty journeys between the latter place and Tádmekkah farther than could be done without such an intimation.

[51] Macrízí, in Hamaker's Specimen Catalogi Cod. Or. MSS. Academiæ Lugd. Bat. pp. 207, 9. In the passage in question M. Hamaker reads Taoumcah تاومكة, instead of which it is an obvious correction to restore Tádmekkah تادمكة. If we

Tádmekkah in the hilly country north of Aghades. It owed its name, signifying the Likeness of Mekkah, to its situation between two hills, in the manner of the Holy City.[52] In the miscellaneous composition of its mercantile population, and in dissolute manners, it was the counterpart of Aúdaghost. Our author adds, that it was nine days from Kaúkaú; but as he appears to be involved in the general mystification enveloping that name, it will be more convenient for the present to waive the consideration of so embarrassing a particular, and to avoid touching on the difficulties attending Kaúkaú till we can make them the immediate subject of discussion.

The route from Ghánah to Tádmekkah leads us again expressly eastward, in the following manner: three days to Safnaḳú, a town on the Nile, and the limit of Ghánah in that direction. Thence along the river to Búgrát, a town of the Merásah. From Búgrát to Tírḳa, and thence over the desert to Tádmekkah.[53]

From all this it appears that the capital of Ghánah was three days distant from the river (at Safnaḳú); and five days from

---

increase forty in the ratio of thirty to fifty, the numbers by which our authors respectively measure the distance between Ghánah and Tádmekkah, we shall have sixty-six days for the distance of the latter place from the Tajúah, according to El Bekrí's scale. The Tajúah or Tajuwín of the Arabs, are the people whom Browne calls Dageou (Travels in Africa, p. 325), and who once ruled Darfur.

[52] The name Tádmekkah signified The Likeness of Mekkah, (Not. et Extr. p. 653.) But Ned Roma, as Leo informs us (pt. IV. c. 6), signified The Likeness of Rome. A single point in Arabic writing discriminates between these two prefixes. But since El Bekrí, who writes Tádmekkah, also writes Nádrúmah, we must be satisfied to ascribe the apparent discrepancy, in this case, to difference of dialect. But it may be here remarked, that the pages of Leo Africanus are not quite free from the inaccuracies which originate in an unpointed Arabic text. They offer, for instance, Perzegreg for Ber Zegzeg, Nefreoa for Nefzeoa, Amarig for Amazig, and frequently Ibn Racu for Ibn Rachic. In the early French translation of Leo (by Jean Temporal, 1556), we find also Cairaran frequently written for Cairaoan, Azarad for Azaoad, and Araran for Araoan. Whether these errors have been all copied from the version of Leo in the first edition of Ramusio's first volume, we have not had the means of determining; but the second edition of Ramusio (1554) is free from the more glaring of them.

[53] Safnaḳú سفنقوا—Búghrát بوغرات MS. B.M. 115 v; Not. et Extr. 652.

Rás el má, or the Head of the Water, where the river issued from the land of the Blacks—that is to say, where it emerged, in its course northwards, from the marshes and dark forests, and laved the open plains of the desert. It thence flowed eastwards, for six days, to Tírḳa, where it turned southwards towards Kaúkaú.

Thus we find the river called by El Bekrí the Nile of the Blacks, described by him throughout its course for above thirty days with a distinctness and completeness of detail quite sufficient to enable us to recognize it with certainty at the present day. If we assume, as we may reasonably do, that Safnaḳú and Ghánah were equidistant from Silla, then from this town to the first-named place was a distance of twenty days. Rás el má stood at least two days further down the stream towards the east or north-east; Tírḳa was therefore twenty-eight days, and the commencement of the country of the Seghmárah thirty-one from Silla.

This winding of a great river, in such a compass, from Negroland northwards to the desert and down again, is a remarkable feature, which cannot be overlooked or mistaken; and it is one which we find in the river of Tomboktú at the present day, exactly as it was described in the river of Ghánah eight centuries ago. And that which renders it more easy to identify the Nile of Ghánah with the Nile of Tomboktú, is the circumstance, that the towns situate at the extremities of the great circuit of the stream comprised within the descriptions of Arab writers, and near the apex of which the emporium of Negroland has always stood, still bear the same names as in ancient times. From the modern Silla, which is evidently identical with the ancient town of that name, a journey of twenty-two days will conduct to the place where the Great River gets clear of the greenland or inundated country and touches the desert, which point is near Tomboktú; thence it flows eastward for six days, and then turns southward or south-eastward to Kaúkaú.[54] Ibn Baṭúṭah, who descended

[54] Silla is fourteen days from Tomboktú by land, and a month by water. From these extremes it is easy to derive the distance assigned above. Sidi Hamed (in Riley's Narrative, p. 334) going from Tomboktú to Houssa, first travelled six days

the river from Tomboktú to Kaúkaú, omits indeed to describe the course of his voyage; but Leo Africanus, who likewise visited those countries, says that Gago, as he writes the name, is four hundred (Italian) miles south by east from Tomboktú.[55] Nor can we doubt that the Gago of Leo is identical with the Kaúkaú of Ibn Baṭúṭah, for Ibn Khaldún expressly informs us that the Kaúkaú here spoken of was also called Kághó.[56]

The exact parallelism of the rivers of Ghánah and Tomboktú, throughout such a length of course, the compared portions being in each case terminated by a Silla on the west, and a Kaúkaú on the east, is of itself quite sufficient to establish their identity with one another. There is, in fact, but one great river on the south side of the Ṣaḥrá to which such descriptions will at all apply. But their resemblance may be traced much further, through a long series of particulars. The Nile of Ghánah was navigated in large boats or barques, just as the river between Jenni and Tomboktú is navigated at the present day.[57] The Berbers inhabiting the shores of the Ṣaḥrá carried their salt and other merchandise in the eleventh century to the Sínghánah, who dwelt on the Great River between Silla and Ghánah: and now they resort in like manner to the banks of the Great River between Silla and Tomboktú.[58] A part of the river between Silla and Ghánah was remarkable as the haunt of hippopotami or river-horses, which animals were killed by the natives, with javelins attached to cords, for the sake of their skins;[59] and Ibn Baṭúṭah, while travelling north-eastward to Tomboktú, probably not far from Jenni, had his attention called to the multitude of those

along the river, a little south of east till he came to hills, where the stream turned southwards.

55 "Verso mezzogiorno, e quasi inchina alla parte di scilocco." Pt. VII. c. 3.

56 The statements of this valuable writer, as well as the journey of Ibn Baṭúṭah, will be given at length further on.

57 Jaubert's Idrísí, in the Rec. de Voy. v. p. 17; Ibn el Wardí.

58 Alexander Scott, in his pilgrimage beyond the Great River, found that the desert continues to the very shores of Lake Debú, where there was a town or encampment of the Orghebets (Raghabát?)—Edinb. Phil. Journ. vol. IV. p. 43.

59 Not. et Extr. p. 640.

animals frequenting the river in the vicinity, and gives a similar account of the means used to destroy them.

Tekrúr, the town or community of Negroland first converted to the Mohammedan faith, was in the neighbourhood of Silla, as already stated, and probably eighteen or twenty days south-west, or south-south-west from Ghánah. It would be, therefore, a decisive proof that this capital stood not far from the position of Tomboktú, if it could be shown that the original site of Tekrúr was near the modern Silla. But to touch this argument here, would be to enter prematurely on the discussion of a question of some magnitude. The application of the name Tekrúr may be more conveniently examined further on, when the historical connexion between Ghánah and Western Negroland shall have been disclosed. For the present it will be sufficient to observe, that the early history of Tekrúr seems to be in a great measure appropriated by the Mandingoes;[60] that the date usually assigned to the conversion of Ghánah, exactly coincides with the epoch of conversion adopted by the Mohammedan nations of western Guinea; and that the glory of the first acceptance of the faith is conceded by undisputed tradition to the country on the Joliba immediately below Silla.[61]

The Nile of Ghánah turned eastward at Rás el má, the most northern part of the river, and not more than five days from Ghánah. Towards that point, therefore, may be said to have been directed the great caravan route from Sijilmésah to Negroland; and now the frequented route from the same quarter conducts to the most northern point of the Great River flowing by Tomboktú, and which, in like manner there turns eastward. It might be added that since the Kaúkaú and Gago, visited from Tomboktú by Ibn Baṭúṭah and Leo, are shown to have been the same place, the distance of 400 Italian miles between that place and Tomboktú, according to the latter writer, agrees perfectly with the distance of fifteen journeys between Ghánah and Kúghah, according to El Bekrí,

---

60 The people of Melli (Málí), according to Leo (pt. VII. c. 4), were the first to embrace the Mohammedan faith.

61 This point will be more fully considered when we come to speak of Tekrúr.

assuming that Kúghah is here written for Kaúkaú or Kághó; but until the peculiarly equivocal character of these names be discussed, no reliance can be placed on any argument involving either of them separately. But they may be dealt with safely when taken together, and where it is not necessary to discriminate between them. Now both El Bekrí and El Edrísí mention Kaúkaú and Kúghah; and if it be conceded that either of these places was identical with the Kaúkaú or Kághó, which, from the 14th to the 18th century, ranked as the most important city in Negroland (a supposition which seems highly probable), then it follows that Ghánah was at least fifteen days higher up the stream, or, according to the construction of the Arab geographers, westward from the same place, which was 400 miles lower down than Tomboktú; and, consequently, was either near the site of the latter city, or, if remote from it, must have been still further westward.

Again, the rivers of Ghánah and Tomboktú closely resemble each other in this respect, that on turning eastward, after attaining their most northern point, they both approach the limits of the Zenágah, whose eastern boundary sloped south-eastward from the road to Ghánah, till, near the river, it reached a distance of ten or twelve days from that capital; and now its relation to Tomboktú may be described in nearly the same terms.[62]

The Nile of the Blacks has been thus traced from Silla, a distance of twenty days north-eastward towards Ghánah; then to a distance of eleven days eastward from the latter place, and then three days southward, where our author's continuous account of its course unfortunately terminates. But we are again led to it by a route through Negroland, so obscure and uncertain indeed as to be in itself of little value; but the discussion of which, as a means of comparing authors, may be indirectly turned to advantage. We are informed by El Bekrí that much of the gold collected in Ghánah was brought from Ghaïárú, eighteen days distant from the former capital, and near the Great River. It is manifest that Ghaïárú did not lie

---

[62] The Brebísh often encamp eastward of Tomboktú, in which quarter nevertheless the Tawárik seem to have gained ground on the Zenágah.

south-westward from Ghánah, for, in that direction, a journey of eighteen days near the river brings us into the vicinity of Tekrúr and Silla, of which our author has already spoken. It must therefore have been situate down the river, below Kaúkaú, or south-eastward from Ghánah; and the described route, not following the stream, must also have gone directly through the interior, till it met the river after its circuit eastward. It seems necessary to suppose that the route does not begin from the capital of Ghánah, but from its frontiers and the opposite side of the river; and also that the day's journey in Negroland was a conventional measure, founded perhaps on the speed of couriers or messengers on horseback, and exceeding that of the loaded caravan in the desert. The construction here given to this route, as described by El Bekrí, agrees in the main with that adopted by subsequent Arab writers, though their misconceptions have in some instances wholly perverted his meaning.[63] The route was as follows:

From Ghánah four days to Sámaḳanda, the inhabitants of which place were the most expert archers among the Blacks. Thence two days to Ṭáḳah; one day more to the branch of the Nile called Zúghú, fordable by camels, but which men were obliged to cross in boats.[64] Thence to Gharnatil or

---

[63] It is a strong argument in favour of the construction here given to the route to Ghaïárú غيارو (MS. B.M. 1120), that it establishes a uniform and consistent method in El Bekrí's narrative. That author begins his account of Negroland with the Ṣínghánah, who traded with the Benú Goddálah in the west. He then goes to the south-west to Silla and Tekrúr; then having mentioned Ghánah, he passes to the route to Ghaïárú, and finally turns due east, and describes the route to Tádmekkah. It is requisite for clearness and exact order, that the route to Ghaïárú should lie between the south-west and the east.

[64] Sámaḳanda سامقندي MS. B.M. 113 r; Sámaghondi سامغندي Rec. de Voy. II. p. 4. The corruptions of this name, which is probably significant, are enumerated in the notes to Hartmann's Idrísí, p. 42.—Ṭáḳah طاقة MS. B.M.; Ṭáḳat طاقت Rec. de Voy. p. 5; Tanah, Not. et Extr. p. 646.—Zúgú زوغوا MS. B.M.; Zoghárá زغارا Rec. de Voy.; Rougou, Not. et Extr.

Ghúntil, an extensive and powerful country wherein Mohammedans experienced good treatment, but had no establishment.[65] Elephants and giraffes were there numerous. From Ghúntil the route went directly to Ghaïárú, a town twelve miles from the Nile. In the latter place, as well as in Bersana, a town on the Nile westward of Ghaïárú, were many Mohammedans, chiefly engaged, it would appear, in the slave trade.[66] "Beyond Bersana, and at the other side of the river," says El Bekrí, "is a great country, eight days in extent, the king of which is called Daúr, and beyond it is

---

65 Gharnatil غرنتل MS. B.M.; Garbil, Not. et Extr. عونتل Oúntil, Rec. de Voy. This latter reading brings to mind the place called by Mohammed Maséní (Clapperton's Second Journey, p. 330), Oodel or Goodel (with the same doubtful initial letter), where the Great River is crossed between Sokkatú and Maséna. In the absence of better guidance, Ghúntil غونتل shall be here assumed to be the true reading, and the name of the identical place called Goodel by Bello's servant.

66 The MS. B.M. fol. 113, has Yersana يرسني, which seems too violently opposed to the other MSS. In the Rec. de Voy. and Not. et Extr. it is Bersa برسي. —This is the Berísa بريسي of Idrísí, the Berísá بريسا of Abulfedá. Bersana was the resort of certain negroes who brought gold from the interior, and were called Benú Námrát بنو نعمرات (Rec. de Voy. p. 7), or Wangamranah ونعمرانه (Not. et Extr. p. 647), or Benú Zammakhrátah بنو زمخراتة (MS. B.M. 113 v). It is plain that the text translated in the Not. et Extr. has been curtailed of the first two letters of the name, but if these be supplied, together with the diacritic points, it agrees with the text of the Rec. de Voy. The name, therefore, will be Benú Námrátah, or Namrát. But who can be the negroes bearing such a name? Sultan Bello informs us, (Appendix to Denham and Clapperton's Travels, vol. II. p. 454) that the people of Yarba or Yariba "originated from the remnants of the children of Canaan, who were of the tribe of Nimrod." The people of Yariba therefore seem to be the Benú Námrát. But to this it may be objected that Námrát is not the correct Arabic mode of writing Nimrod. Truly not; neither can the blacks of Yariba, we verily believe, prove their descent from the great hunter. But the name and the historical tradition in this case are both equally spurious; they were both probably suggested by a sound—we think indeed, by the same sound, or, in other words, we believe that the name which was shaped into Benú Námrát, and afterwards into Benú Nemrúd or descendants of Nimrod, belonged to the people of Yariba.

Melil or Malelo, the king of which is a true believer, while his people are still Pagans." We may suppose the countries here mentioned to be the Daúri and Mallawa of modern geography, the former northward of Kanó, extending towards the desert, the latter a large region, comprising apparently in the acceptation of the indigenous population, the north-western portion of the country called Houssa.[67] But it must be acknowledged that little confidence is due to conjectures guided only by such obscure and equivocal indications.

Among the countries depending on Ghánah, according to El Bekrí, was Sámah, four days distant from Ghánah. Its inhabitants, who were called the Bokmo, used poisoned arrows, and were reckoned the best archers among the blacks. In this circumstance, as well as in their distance from Ghánah, they resemble the people of Sámaḳanda; so that we are led at once to suspect that the latter place was the metropolis of Samah.[68] But it is a curious coincidence that a people named Bokmo should be at a short distance from Ghánah, towards the south, and that a district called Bagamo should have a similar position with respect to Tomboktú. For Marmol, copying the words of De Barros with a few slight additions, thus expresses himself respecting the various names of the rivers of Tomboktú, in conformity with the erroneous opinion prevalent in his time, that it flowed into the sea by the Senegal. "The Portuguese (he

---

[67] Daur دور Not. et Extr. p. 647; Daú دوْ MS. B.M. fol. 113 v.; Dawa دَوَ Rec. de Voy. II. p. 7.—Malelo مَلُل MS. B.M.; Malik مَلْك Rec. de Voy. For the various readings of the names Ghaïárú (Ganarah of D'Herbelot) and Ghuntil, see Hartmann's Edrísí.

[68] In the Kissour language, spoken, according to Caillié, in Tomboctú, Jenni, and in the intervening country, the word Ganda (Caillié III. p. 313), or Gunda (Clapperton's First Journey, p. 182), signifies Land or Country, so that Samaḳanda or Samaghondi, explained by it, would mean Samah-land. Nor is this explanation less probable from the circumstance that the name Sami, and the termination Kanda or Konda, signifying town, is common among the Mandingoes, who overwhelmed Ghánah from the south, as shall be shown hereafter, and who now people the country south of Tomboktú (Caillié, tom. II. 252).

says) call it Zenega; the Zenagas, Zenedec; the Gelofes, Dengueh: the Tucorones, further in, call it Mayo; the Saragoles, higher up, name it Colle; and when it goes through a district called *Bagamo*, more to the east, they call it Zimbala; in the kingdom of Tombut it is called Yça."[69] The name Zimbala or Jimbala has always hovered in the neighbourhood of Tomboktú and vicinity of the river. Its exact position has been matter of controversy. Yet there seems little reason for dissenting from the statement of Caillié, who says that a large tract of country south of Tomboktú bears that name.[70] The tract in question therefore must be on the eastern bank of the river between lake Debú and Tomboktú, and there also we must look for Bagamo.[71]

---

[69] Marmol (vol. III. fol. 17). Yça, that is, Issa, (Hissa in Caillié's vocabulary) signifies *river* in the language of Tomboktú. The Serakholies inhabit Galam. The Tucorones therefore interposed between them and the Wolofs, must be the Fúlah or Fellatah, who occupy both banks of the Senegal, in the neighbourhood of the Isle de Morfil. We find in a MS. vocabulary of their language, brought home by Clapperton, the word *mio* signifying a lake, probably any large sheet of water. With respect to the name here applied to them, a respectable authority (Dard, Grammaire Wolofe, p. 148) informs us, that a division of the Fúlah nation bears the appellation of Teukirères. The name Tucorones seems related to the plural Tekayrne, used by Burckhardt (Trav. in Nubia, p. 365); while Teukirères rather resembles the Tekrírí of Ibn Baṭúṭah. It is manifest that the route pointed out by this series of names is that of the slave-dealers between Galam and Tomboktú. They cross the desert at a distance from the Great River where it is called Joliba, and first reach the stream where it turns eastward, north of Lake Debú. There, according to Bowdich's informant (Mission to Ashantee, p. 193), Jinbala is on the left bank of the river. It is placed on the right by all other authorities except Marmol and his copiers, who give the name to the river.

[70] Caillié's account of Jimbala, or, as he writes it, Ginbala, was confirmed by Abú Bekr, the intelligent native of Tomboktú who accompanied Mr. Davidson in his ill fated attempt to cross the desert from Wád Nún; and of whom an interesting account may be read in the Journal of the Royal Geographical Society, vol. VI. p. 100. The initial sound in Jimbala is one hard to be seized by a foreign ear. It is the same which Caillié (II. pp. 82, 160) sought to express by a triple form in Jaulas, Diaulas, and Iolas. Park wrote the same name Jules (First Journey), while Mr. Watt preferred Nyalas (Proc. Afr. Ass. I. 436). The natives themselves often express the sound in question by y'e يج.

The King styled Ghánah, while residing in Aúdaghost, aided, we are told, the King of Másín in a war of the latter with the King of Aúghám. But it appears that the last-named place was close to Aúkár, subsequently the capital of Ghánah, and was passed through in going from that city to Rás el má. One of the belligerent parties being thus found near Ghánah and the river, it is natural that we should look for the other in the same neighbourhood; and the conjecture seems as unobjectionable as it is obvious, that the Másín of El Bekrí is the Másín or Maséna of the present time, situate on the western side of the Great River, not far north from Silla.[72] The same writer tells us that to the west of Ghánah was the hostile country of Anbárah, nine days from Kúghah, which was fifteen from Ghánah. This statement presents insuperable difficulties; inasmuch as it contradicts the general testimony which places Ghánah at the extreme west of the Black nations on the frontiers of Negroland, and because by referring to Kúghah it introduces the confusion accompanying that name. If, however, we boldly solve the problem by supposing Kúghah to be written for Kaúkaú or Kághó, and by placing Anbárah accordingly south by east from Ghánah, we shall then recognize it in the warlike state of Oonbori, situate in the Hajri or mountainous country south of Tomboktú.[73]

---

[71] Marmol elsewhere (III. fol. 27 r) distinctly places the *Baganos* on the river at the point where the road from Galam to Tomboktú first reaches its banks. Livio Sanuto also (Geografia, 1588, fol. 83) says, "that Zimbala or *Bagano* adjoins Tomboktú on the south, beyond the Sanaga," that is, the Great River. Mohammed Maséní (Clapperton, p. 331) mentions a lake Búkma as being in the same tract as Lake Jeboo, that is, Dhiebú or Debú.

[72] Not. et Extr. p. 617. Másín ماسين MS. B.M. fol. 103. For Aúghám, see page 29. The Massina of our maps, and Maséna of the Translations appended to Clapperton's Second Journey, is generally written Másín or Máshín by the natives (see the documents appended to Bowdich's Mission, and to Dupuís' Residence in Ashantee).

[73] Anbarah أَنْبَارَة Rec. de Voy. p. 8. The king of this country was styled Tárim تَارِم. If for this we could read Farim فارم, we should have a true Man-

But an anonymous Arab writer expresses himself more intelligibly respecting the political relations of Ghánah; he says that twenty parasangs or leagues east of that city was Ráyún, or perhaps rather Ráyawen, the nearest city (on the southern border) of the desert, to Sijilmésah and Wergelán. Between Ráyawen and Ghánah were the encampments of the Morabites, with whom the people of the latter place waged war, as well as with the inhabitants of Amímah, a town, as has been already observed, not far from Tomboktú towards the west or south-west.[74]

Of the laws and usages of Ghánah, such as were capable of enduring after subjection to a foreign power and conversion to the Mohammedan faith, but scanty notices have been transmitted to us. It deserves to be remarked, nevertheless, that the law of inheritance in Ghánah gave the preference to the sister's son, and that the same law remained in force in the fourteenth century in Waláta, as well as in the Mandingo kingdom of Málí, where, however, its existence need not create

---

dingo title. The difference between Anbárah أنبارة and Oonbori, probably أنبري supposing the vowels not to have been supplied conjecturally, (for otherwise the latter might be read Anbara,) is no greater than may be expected where orthography is unsettled. The title of the king of Oonbori is Farma (Clapperton's Second Journey, p. 331), which, as well as Farim, imports a governor or local chief.

That by Kúghah كوغة (Rec. de Voy.) El Bekrí meant the Cochia of Cadamosto (Ramusio, I. fol. 108 v) and Gago of Leo, can hardly be doubted; but this point shall be examined hereafter. His statement, that Anbárah, nine days from Kúghah, west of Ghánah, does not admit of any plausible defence; but if Sámah سامة be read in this place for Ghánah غانة then not only does all difficulty vanish, but the author's discourse acquires coherence and natural order.

[74] Kitábu-l-Járáfíah (Book of Geography), &c. MS. in the collection of D. Pascual de Gayangos. Ráyawen رايون has a suspicious resemblance to Arawan. It is quite gratuitous to suppose that the Morabites, who were all of the Zenágah nation, and who rushed at once, as soon as they felt their strength, from their own deserts to the conquest of Barbary and Spain, ever went eastward as far as Houssa, or even to Kághó.

surprise.[75] But in Waláta, on the border of the desert, with a population chiefly of Berber origin, the existence of a law so singular, so characteristic of Guinea, and so exactly coinciding with the law of Ghánah, strongly argues the influence of Negro rule, and favours the presumption arising out of what precedes, that Waláta was comprised within the limits of Ghánah.

One of the customs of Ghánah, transiently mentioned by El Bekrí, calls for some remark. In the presence of the king, the people prostrated themselves, and sprinkled their naked bodies with dust. This agrees exactly with what Ibn Baṭúṭah witnessed and justly reprobated at the court of Málí.[76] Such slavish manners could never have originated on the border of the desert, nor where local circumstances give the least encouragement to the love of independence. They are the manners of Western Guinea, and cannot be supposed to have ever existed in Houssa, a hilly country, divided into petty states, each cherishing a rude spirit of liberty. Succession to power in Houssa, is said to be elective among the sons; the hereditary principle being thus blended with the exercise of a popular right.[77] In Bornú it has been always customary to consult the dignity of the sovereign by concealing him from the vulgar gaze, and not by debasing the subject. Those admitted to the presence of the king sit with their backs to the curtain which screens the royal person.[78]

---

75 "No one (in Aïwalátin, that is, Walata) is named after his father, but after his maternal uncle; and the sister's son always succeeds to property in preference to the son: a custom I witnessed nowhere else except among the infidel Hindoos of Malabar." (Lee's Ibn Baṭúṭah, p. 234.)

76 "Of all people the Blacks debase themselves most in presence of their king... When the Sultan addresses one of them, he (who is addressed) will take the garment off his back and throw dust upon his head" (Lee's Ibn Baṭúṭah, p. 240). The ceremonial of Tomboktú (Leo, pt. VII. c. 5), and that of Ghánah (Not. et Extr. p. 644), are described in nearly the same terms.

77 Proc. of Afr. Assoc. I. p. 149. Though Clapperton says little of the laws or government of Houssa, yet his narrative discloses the subdivision of power in that country. The people there have never been trained up under a paramount tyranny.

78 Makrízí (Quatremère, Mémoires sur la Nubie, tom. I. p. 28; Burckhardt's Travels in Nubia, p. 456) relates of the court of Kánem, and Ibn Baṭúṭah of that of Bornú, the ceremony of audience, as it was witnessed in the latter place by Denham (I. p. 231).

In El Bekrí's time the dominion of Ghánah extended toward the east but three days' journey from the capital. Toward the south it could not have reached very far. The independent kingdom of Tekrúr was, at the utmost, eighteen or twenty days distant in that direction. Still nearer was Ṣinghánah, apparently an independent state, which carried on trade with the Benú Goddálah. This trade was guided in its channel, as must always be the case in the early stages of society, by natural circumstances. A branch of the desert penetrates south-eastward to the very banks of the Great River, in a tract of which we know not the exact width, but which embraces the western shores of Lake Debú.[79] Such a road, laid open by nature, could not fail to exert a great influence on the history of Negroland. And indeed, the fact that Tekrúr, situate near that part of the river, was the first converted of the Negro states; that the trade of the Berbers occupying the sea shore at Aúlíl, and subsequently their sway also, extended to the same quarter, might alone create a suspicion, that the tribes of the desert found in that tract of country a nature congenial to their habits. This suspicion is converted into certainty by the narrative of Alexander Scott, who crossed the tract in question.[80] The Berbers were actual possessors of territory south of Ghánah, where the desert approached the Great River between that country and Tekrúr. North of Ghánah, the dry desert of Tíser or Azawad was but eight or ten days distant. In that direction, however, as well as towards the

---

[79] Caillié saw (Voy. II. p. 253) a line of hills of red sandstone without any vegetation, on the left bank of the river, about forty miles south of the lake; and, at an equal distance north of it, sand hillocks bordered the stream (p. 266). It is explicitly stated by Marmol (III. fol. 15 v), that Jenni had all the trade of the Zenágah, the Brebísh, the Ludayas, and the Arabs of Arguin. But he erred in supposing that the conflux of Arabs and Berbers from the shores of the Ṣaḥrá to that city was owing to its western position. It was rather due to the character of the intervening country, which may be called a fine desert.

[80] It is plain, from Scott's narrative (Edinb. Phil. Jour. vol. IV. p. 45), that the level desert continues, without any change, save in the frequency of brackish rills, to the very shore of the lake; southwards from which the country seemed uninhabited; but a little to the north was the town of the Orghebets, in which the dwellings were constructed of canes and bamboos.

west, the wilderness opposed no precise limits to the claims of empire, but allowed pretensions of sovereignty to expatiate freely over territories of two months' journey in extent.

Thus we have seen that Ghánah was the frontier kingdom of the Blacks contiguous to the advanced portion of the Great River at its north-west angle; and extending in front of that portion of the desert, over which lay the commerce with Sijilmésah,—a commerce guided by a principle, which if not strictly unchangeable, at least fluctuates only within narrow limits,—namely, that of choosing the shortest and safest route across the desert. It comprised the country between Waláta and the Great River, near the future site of Tomboktú, and enjoyed the identical advantages of position which subsequently made the latter city so prosperous.

But what were the revolutions, it may be asked, which caused Ghánah to disappear? This question shall be fully answered hereafter; our inquiry at present regards the place where Ghánah existed, and not the events which led to its extinction. Yet it will not be alien from our purpose to observe, that although the name, or rather title, of Ghánah became politically extinct, and was erased from the list of sovereignties, yet it still adhered obscurely, in the sixteenth century, to at least one spot of the territory originally designated by it. For Marmol informs us, that in his time Walata was also called Ganata; and that he did not in this instance hazard an erudite conjecture, but spoke the plain language of habit and experience, is evident as well from the unostentatiousness of the remark, as from the frequency with which he indifferently employs these two names one for the other.[81]

---

[81] "*Gualata*, que otros llaman *Ganata*." Marmol, III. fol. 21 v. It is hardly necessary to observe, that, in the orthography of Southern Europe, Gualata represents our Walata: "*Gualata* o *Ganata*," (I. fol. 17.) "Vled Vodey andan en los desiertos que estan entre Iguaden y *Ganata;* son señores de Iguaden, y el Rey Negro de *Ganata* les paga cierto tributo," &c. (I. fol. 39.) "Alarabes llamados Udaya, y por otro nombre Vled Vodey, que moran el desierto de Lybia que está entre esta poblacion (Guaden) y *Gualata* reyno de negros." (III. fol. 3.) "En Gelofe, Geneúa, Tombuto, Meli, Gago y *Ganata*, hablan una lengua llamada Zungay." (I. fol. 44.) This last sentence is taken from Leo (pt. I. c. 11), who,

Let the reader now recal the account of Negroland, and of Ghánah in particular, given in the preceding pages; let him fix his attention on those features of the description pointed out for the purpose of showing that Ghánah was near the site of Tomboktú; let him consider well that those features have a magnitude incompatible with the supposition of their being repeated, and a permanence derived from their dependence on the physical constitution of the African continent. Let him, in fact, figure to himself a great and navigable river, flowing from a town called Silla north-eastwards for three weeks, through the country of the Blacks who first embraced the Mohammedan faith, skirting the desert eastwards for six days, and then turning southwards to a place called Kaúkaú, or Kághó; let him place the emporium of Negroland near the north-western angle of that river, at a distance of two months' ordinary travelling from the shores of the Atlantic, two months from Sijilmésah, and fifty days from Tádmekkah, not far from the modern Aghades. He may then trace the road from Sijilmésah to that emporium, dividing the whole distance into its distinct portions, viz.—eleven days south-westward to the border of the desert, then six days over the hills, about seventeen more to the zone of drifting sand, passing near the salt mines of Tagháza, and eight or ten over an utterly inhospitable tract near the southern limit of the Ṣaḥrá. Along this road he may distribute the tents of the wandering Masúfah; and, a little to the east of it, he may mark the boundary line of the great Berber nation, the Zenágah. Let him

---

however, writes Gualata. Marmol, in his first volume, seems to prefer Ganata, but, in the third, he generally follows Leo with little deviation. When Ali Bey (Badia) speaks of caravans going "from Sús and Táfílélt to Ghánah and Tomboktú," (Travels in Barbary, &c. I. 45,) does he inadvertently mix ancient with modern times—his reading with his recent intelligence?—or does he mean by Ghánah, Ghanata, that is, Walata? What was surmised in Note 2 respecting the predominance gained by the analogies of the Berber language over those of the Arabic, and the change of the contingent ṯ into the absolute t, seems confirmed by the MS. extract of El Bekrí published in the Rec. de Voy. II. That MS., however inferior in other respects, is yet good authority on the subject of the relation subsisting between ancient Arabic and Moorish orthography; and we find that it writes Ghánat, Sámat, and Ṭáḳat, for Ghánaṯ or Ghánah, Sámaṯ, Ṭáḳaṯ, &c.

then write above Silla, on the left hand, this remark:—"Trade carried on with the Berbers on the sea shore;" and below Kaúkaú, on the right,—"Obscure and little known:"[82] and when, having finished this delineation, he finds that, though drawn in conformity with the descriptions of Ghánah, it is yet perfectly applicable to Tomboktú; and that it is equally true and faithful, whichever of these names be given to the emporium of the Blacks: then, even if he throw aside all other considerations, such as the relations of Ghánah with the Morabites and with Mímah, the town whence Tomboktú derived its Berber population, he certainly cannot refuse to admit that the Ghánah of Arab writers was contiguous to that part of the Great River where Tomboktú now stands.

In the sixteenth and seventeenth centuries, when numerous accounts of Barbary were published in Europe, and when the trade of Morocco and Táfílélt (the ancient Sijilmésah) with Negroland was highly rated, we find that, besides Tomboktú, whither the routes from Táfílélt and Wád Nún conducted, no places of any importance in Negroland were mentioned, except Jenni near Silla, and Gago, which is the same as Kaúkaú. The caravans across the desert directed their march to the nearest point of Negroland, and the merchants, arriving there, never looked beyond the marts with which they could thence maintain a direct intercourse. In the same manner, and exactly within the same limits, was El Bekrí's information circumscribed. He says nothing of the Mandingoes, Serakholies, Wolofs, Fellatah, or other black nations of the west. He is equally silent respecting Houssa, toward the south-east. Of Kánem, which was reckoned to be only forty days distant

---

[82] "It appears singular that the country immediately to the eastward of Timbuctoo as far as Kashna should be more imperfectly known to the Moorish traders than the rest of central Africa" (Quart. Rev. No. 45, May 1820, p. 234.) The reviewer, however, errs in ascribing the obscurity which involves that tract to the wars of the Fellatah. But the fact is, that between Tomboktú and Houssa passes the line of demarcation separating what may be called the two commercial provinces of Negroland, which depend on the two great roads (from Fezzán and Táfílélt), and have little communication with each other on their northern frontiers. Besides, the interposed desert supports a formidable population of Tawárik.

from Zawílah, he speaks in terms indicative of the faintness of his knowledge:—"The people," he says, "are blacks and idolators; and the country is hardly ever visited by travellers." —Thus the analogous modes in which Ghánah and Tomboktú present themselves respectively to the ancient and modern historians of Negroland, corroborate the opinion that the site of the former of those places was in the vicinity of the latter.[83]

In the attempt here made to demonstrate that Ghánah was near the site of Tomboktú, it will be perceived that no aid has been sought from etymologies or fancied resemblance of names; much less have such delusive lights been allowed to guide our investigations. The arguments urged in the foregoing pages rest wholly on necessary deductions from the obvious sense of our Arab authorities, without any attempt to wrest their meaning. The topics touched on in those arguments may be thus briefly recapitulated:

The description of Ghánah in respect to its bearing and distance from Sijilmésah—the details of the road to it, and characteristics of the desert—the relations of Ghánah with the Zenágah, and particularly with the Morabites—its intercourse with the tribes on the sea shore—the position of Genéwah—the course of the River—the relations of Ghánah with Mimah, Másín or Masena, Anbárah, &c.—the name Ganata remaining to Walata—the laws and usages of Ghánah.

There still remains an argument of no common weight, the substance of which, though belonging to another part of this inquiry, yet may, without impropriety, be briefly stated here. The Blacks of the country named Málí, who, it will be seen, were Mandingoes, issuing from the south-west, conquered

---

[83] The Arab geographers, unable to form an exact conception of the country westward of Ghánah, diminished the distance between that place and the ocean. El Idrísí makes the distance between Silla and Aúlíl to be sixteen days' journey (Rec. de Voy. v. p. 11); but Abulfedá sets Ghánah only four degrees eastward of the ocean (Reiske's Trans. in Büsching's Mag. v. p. 354). In like manner Leo (pt. VII. c. 3) says that the kingdom of Jenni, extending 250 miles along the river, reaches the ocean; and he supposes Walata to be only a hundred miles from the sea shore. As he was copied in all his errors, our maps of the sixteenth and seventeenth centuries uniformly placed Tomboktú too far westward.

Ghánah. Their empire (to use the words of their historian) extended from Ghánah in the east, to the ocean in the west. Nearly a century after that conquest, they advanced eastward (or rather south-eastward) to Kaúkaú, whence they marched into the desert and made themselves masters of Tekaddá. They subsequently relinquished, however, the possession of that place, and retired to Kaúkaú; so that the Great River formed the boundary of their sway towards the east, with the exception, perhaps, of a short space below Kaúkaú. Now there can be no uncertainty respecting the ground over which these conquerors marched. The celebrated traveller, Ibn Baṭúṭah, visited, in the fourteenth century, the capital of Málí, on the Joliba above Sego; he thence travelled to Tomboktú; thence descended the river to Kaúkaú, and from that place he went to Tekaddá, which was on the road from Kaúkaú to Ghát and Ghodémis. He thus appears to have followed exactly the course which had been taken by the Mandingo conquerors; the only difference in his described route being, that he found Tomboktú where they had found Ghánah.

EL IDRISI COMPARED WITH EL BEKRI.

MAGHRAWAH.

The account of Negroland contained in the foregoing pages is drawn altogether from El Bekrí. So much does his description of Ghánah and the adjoining countries excel in copiousness of detail as well as in clearness, that in all the Arab writers succeeding him, there is hardly a single new particular worth adding to it. Some of these writers, nevertheless, are much better known than El Bekrí; and one of them, El Idrísí, whose work, entitled 'The Amusement of one desirous of knowing all the Countries of the World,' was composed about the year 1153, has been long regarded as the first authority on questions relating to the geography of Central Africa. It will be worth while, therefore, to set these two authors side by side, and to compare them carefully, so that we may be able to choose between them when they disagree, and to determine whether the later of the two improved on his precursor.

The first peculiarity of El Idrísí that strikes the attentive reader, is his general reduction of distances in the desert. He begins to contract even in the vicinity of Atlas, and makes Sijilmésah to be only thirteen days distant from Wád Nún; whereas these places must be at least twenty good journeys asunder.[84] But to confine ourselves to the consideration of the principal dimensions of the Ṣaḥrá, we may recal the statement of El Bekrí that Aúlíl was a two months' journey distant from Wád Nún, going along the shore. Now from Sijilmésah to Aúlíl, which was a greater distance, is reckoned by El Idrísí to be a journey of only forty days. This supposes (since Arguín is exactly 900 miles from Sijilmésah) a rate of 22½ geographical miles a day in a straight line—a rate far exceeding what is practicable on a journey of such a nature and extent.[85] Nor can El Idrísí have here the benefit of any objection to the hypothesis which places Aúlíl at Arguín, since he informs us that Aúlíl was one day's sail from the mouth of the river called the Nile of the Blacks, by which he must be understood to mean the Senegal. But the mouth of this river is at least two days' sail from Arguín; so that to make that author consistent with himself, it must be allowed not only that Aúlíl was in

---

[84] El Idrísí places Nún, or as he writes it, Núl, at a distance of three days from the sea, and thirteen (erroneously reduced to three by Hartmann) from Sijilmésah (Rec. de Voy. v. p. 205). But the town of Wád Nún is one or two days (22 miles) from the sea (Davidson's Notes), twelve from Tatta, and sixteen from the chief town of Daráh (Proc. of Afr. Assoc. I. p. 224), which is six days from Sijilmésah (Jackson's Shabeeny, p. 3). The last-named place must, therefore, be twenty-two days from Wád Nún, and twenty-three, at least, from the sea. In like manner El Idrísí reduces to three and eight days respectively the distances of Sijilmésah from Daráh and Aghmát, which El Bekrí, confirmed by modern itineraries, estimates at six and fourteen days.

[85] Major Rennell, in his 'Memoir on the rate of Travelling as performed by Caravans' (Phil. Trans. Vol. LXXXI. p. 144), concludes that in Africa fourteen geographical miles and five-sixths of horizontal distance, is the mean daily rate of loaded caravans. M. Walckenaer (Recherches, &c. p. 266,) adopts fifteen geographical miles as the ordinary rate.

the Bay of Arguin, but also that his numerical expressions of distance are, in this instance, too low.[86] In like manner he reduces the distance between Sijilmésah and Silla to forty days; and that from Wád Nún to the latter place to thirty-two days,—viz. seven from Nún to Arkí, and thence twenty-five to Silla; his estimate in each case being less than two-thirds of the reality.[87]

But the same author's reduction of the longitudinal dimensions of the Great Desert is still more remarkable. Instead of a journey of two months between Aúlíl and Silla, as may be inferred from El Bekrí, whose measures of distance accord strictly with the results of modern inquiry, El Idrísí separates those places by a distance of only sixteen days. Again, he makes Aúdaghost to be but a month from Aúlíl, and twenty-five days from Jermah in Fezzán; so that from the latter place to the shores of the Atlantic, the desert should be crossed in fifty-five days, or less than half of the time actually required for that journey.[88] Again, he states Kúghah to be a month from Dongolah, and six weeks from Ghánah (though the genuineness of the text is here liable to suspicion); and consequently he

---

86 From Cape St. Anne in the Bay of Arguin, to the mouth of the Senegal, is a distance of 260 nautical miles, or about forty hours of moderate sailing.

87 Rec. de Voy. pp. 12, 206. Arkí (see Note 34) appears under various forms in the copies of El Idrísí: as Arḳi ارقى Rec. de Voy. pp. 12, 107; Azḳi ازقى; Azki ازكى Ibid. p. 206, and in the Abridgment. Ibn el Wardi also writes Azki, which, he says, is the place where travellers (ascending the Desert from Wád Nún) begin to climb the rocks (Not. et Extr. II. p. 23). Ibn Baṭúṭah travelled forty-five days from Sijilmésah to Aïwalátin, or Walata, whence Silla cannot be less than twenty days' distant. From the latter place to Wád Nún is now reckoned a journey of fifty-five days (Davidson's Notes, &c.).

88 From the capital of Fezzán to Tomboktú is reckoned a journey of three months (Lyon, Travels in N. Afr. p. 144); or to calculate more accurately, from Morzúk to Twát is a distance of thirty-nine or forty days, and thence to Tomboktú, is a journey of forty-five or forty-seven days (Walckenaer, Rech. p. 423; Quart. Rev. No. 45, p. 230). If to the sum of eighty-four days thus found, be added the journey of two months, or rather two months and a half, between Tomboktú and the sea (see Note 37), we shall have for the distance between Fezzán and the ocean nearly three times the space assigned by El Idrísí; and, reducing the route to a straight line, with all possible allowance, more than double.

reduces the whole distance between Dongolah, or the Nile in the east, and the Atlantic Ocean in the west, to a journey of three months and a half, which is not more than a moiety of the true distance.[89]

The incorrectness of El Idrísí exemplified above, cannot be explained away by supposing that he made use of a large scale of measures, or a conventional day's journey of great length. His contraction of space is not sufficiently uniform to sustain that plea: it operates chiefly on the uninhabited country. Like modern geographers, he seems to have had an invincible dislike to large blanks in a map; and among the expedients to which he had recourse for the purpose of filling them up, was the common one of dilating as much as possible the contiguous inhabited countries. A perfect illustration of this remark is afforded by his description of the course of the Great River in the vicinity of Ghánah.

It has been seen that El Bekrí places the capital of Ghánah not immediately on the Great River, but at a distance of perhaps three days' journey from it. But Ṣínghánah, with which place he begins his description of Negroland, is described by him as standing on both banks of the river, and having Tekrúr on the south-west. Now in El Idrísí's geography there is no mention made of Ṣínghánah, but its description is trans-

---

89 The text stating the distance of Kúghah from Ghánah to be a month and a half, occurs in the Abridgment of El Idrísí (Hartmann's Idrísí, p. 42), but is wanting in the larger work. There is good reason for believing it to be an interpolation. From Ghánah to Seghmárah, according to El Idrísí, was eighteen days ; thence to Sámakanda eight days ; and thence to Kúghah ten days. So that if these places be all arranged in a straight line from west to east, Kúghah will be still only thirty-six days from Ghánah, instead of forty-five. But while El Idrísí expressly traces eastwards the route from Ghánah to Seghmárah, and sets Kúghah eastward of Sámakanda, he says nothing of the bearing of Sámakanda from Seghmárah ; so that we are at liberty to set the former place west by south from the latter, under the guidance of El Bekrí, whose Sámakanda was only four days from Ghánah. The two authors will then be found to coincide in general design, and El Idrísí's Kúghah will be not above twenty days from Ghánah. It would be easy, were it worth while, to explain why the epitomator, trying to supply an apparent deficiency in his author's ill-connected details, should have separated Kúghah from Ghánah by a month and a half's journey.

ferred to Ghánah, which is made to stand on both banks of the river, and to have Tekrúr on the south-west. The distance of twenty days, according to El Bekrí, between Silla and Ghánah, is increased by El Idrísí to twenty-four days. The former of these writers thus describes the route eastward and along the river from Ghánah. First, five days to Rás el má, then six days through the country of the Merásah to Tírḳa, where the river turned southwards, and three days further along its banks, to the country of the Seghmárah, which commenced, therefore, at the distance of fourteen days from Ghánah. The same course is thus described by El Idrísí:—From Ghánah, six or eight days to Tírḳa; six more to Merásah; and another six to Seghmárah: so that the fourteen days of his author are here increased to eighteen.[90]

In accordance with the construction given above to El Bekrí's route from Ghánah to Ghaïárú, El Idrísí makes the portion of the river therein mentioned to form a part of its course below Seghmárah. But the manner in which the latter writer puts together his materials in this place demands attentive consideration. The following are his details of distance and bearing:—

From Samghadah (Sámaḳanda)	to Seghmárah,		8 days.
From ditto	to Kúghah,	*eastwards,*	10
From ditto	to Gharbíl (Ghúntil),		9
From Seghmárah	to Gharbíl,	*southwards,*	6
From Gharbíl (Ghúntil)	to Ghanárah (Ghaïárú),	*westwards,*	11
From Ghánah	to Ghanárah,		11

Thus it appears that El Idrísí makes the river flow first north-eastward from Silla to Ghánah; then eastwards to Seghmárah; then southwards to Ghúntil, and finally westwards again to Ghaïárú.

The Sámaḳanda of El Bekrí, which was four days from

---

90 From Silla to Berísa, according to El Idrísí, was twelve days; thence to Ghánah twelve days; or to Aúdaghost twelve days; and between the two last-named places twelve days. This is a handsome arrangement. Again, from Ghánah to Tírḳa six days; thence to Merásah six days; thence to Seghmárah six days; thence to Ghúntil six days. Then come distances of eight, nine, ten, and eleven days. These numbers alone are enough to excite suspicion.

Ghánah, and his Kúghah, fifteen days from the same capital, and nine from Anbárah, (which appears to have been near Sámaḳanda,) are evidently the Samghadah and Kúghah of El Idrísí. This writer agrees with his predecessor in making the river flow, first north-eastwards from Silla to Ghánah, then eastwards, and then southwards. So far he seized with some felicity the idea of the general winding of the river. But his turning it westward from Ghúntil can be explained only by supposing that he misunderstood his authority. El Bekrí says, that opposite to the Seghmárah, whose territory extended from the Great River to Tádmekkah, was Kaúkaú. And again, he remarks, that the road to the country of the Remrem went

The River according to El Bekrí.

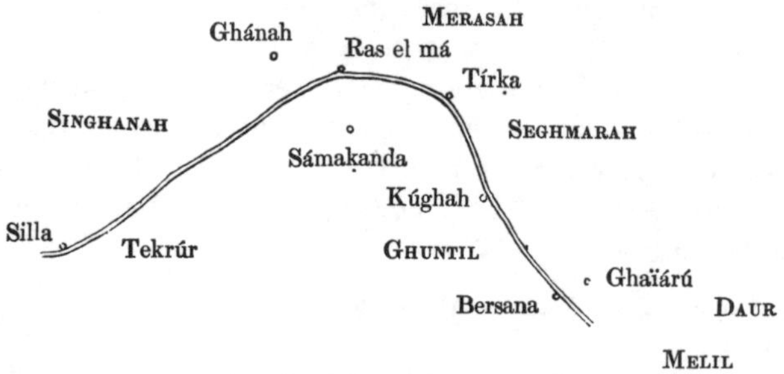

westwards along the river from Kaúkaú. Now this last passage furnishes the explanation of the westward course which El Idrísí has given to the river, if we suppose that he confounded for a moment Kúghah with Kaúkaú.

El Bekrí mentions Bersana after Ghaïárú; and accordingly El Idrísí sets this place, under the altered name of Berísa, due west of Ghaïárú, and on the Great River, half way between Silla and Ghánah. The series of names which the latter found in his author he thus arranged in a circle, under the influence of misconception, so as to make it terminate in itself. But the artificial division of climates, by severing Berísa from the group of names to which it originally belonged, fortunately obviated the ready exposure of so absurd a concatenation.[91] The

[91] The Berísa of El Idrísí is the same place of which the name is written in the

Malilo and Daúr or Daú of El Bekrí are evidently the Malel and Daú of El Idrísí; and in consequence of the same mistake which placed Berísa on the river between Ghánah and Silla, they are brought into the neighbourhood of the latter place. Their character, too, is as much misrepresented as their position. Instead of being countries of some extent and importance, they become, in the pages of El Idrísí, only towns of Lemlem, the wretched inhabitants of which, possessing but few camels, wander over deserts destitute of water;—a picture of Negro poverty, more likely it must be confessed, to originate in the imagination of an Arab, than in the physical character of the country south of the Great River.

The River according to El Idrísí.

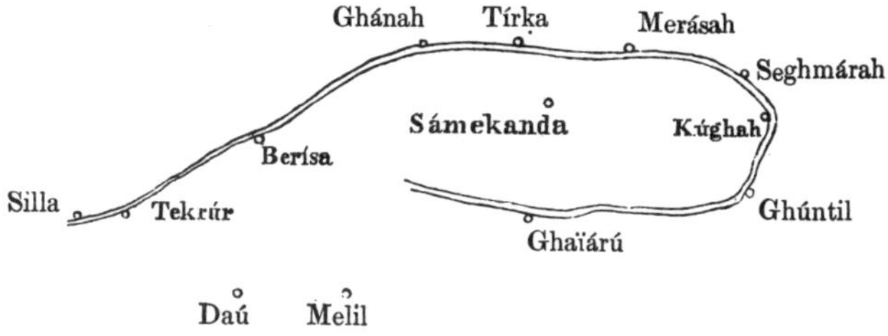

From El Idrísí's delineation of the Great River we may return with advantage to consider the position assigned by him to Aúdaghost. That town was, according to him, thirty days from Aúlíl, thirty-one from Wergelán, and twenty-five from Jermah. The short distance of fifty-five days herein allowed between Aúlíl and Jermah, will not admit of being applied to a circuitous route. The distance from Wergelán, therefore, which is relatively long, and by reaching far southwards has the effect of elongating the preceding line, must

copies of El Bekrí, Bersa برسی Not. et Extr. p. 647; Yerma يرمی (rather Yersa يرسی), Rec. de Voy. II. p. 6; and Yersana يرسنی MS. B.M. El Bekrí represents Ghúntil as a great country; he does not state the distance of Ghaïárú from it, but places the latter twelve miles from the river, and Bersana, or Yersana, west of it on the river. But, in El Idrísí, the corresponding names all designate towns which stand eleven or twelve days' journey asunder.

be supposed to be circuitous. And this is a well-founded supposition, inasmuch as the road from Wergelán to Aúdaghost must have passed through Twát, and probably also by Wanzamín. Now the point which satisfies the conditions of distance specified above, and at the same time best eludes surrounding difficulties, will be found to be not far from the 20th parallel of north latitude, and the 1st meridian of east longitude, or about 120 miles east of the position assigned to Aúdaghost in our map. Thus it appears that El Idrísí's statements respecting the position of Aúdaghost, do not, when taken together, lend the slightest countenance to the hypothesis which makes that place identical with Aghades. For that position, deduced in the strictest possible manner from the assigned conditions, still leads to the conclusion that Ghánah was situate on the northern bend of the river of Tomboktú. But since we likewise learn from the same writer, that it was situate on the western, and not the eastern portion of that northern bend, we have no alternative but to correct his distances with respect to the angle of the river, and to remove Aúdaghost further west, so as to place it exactly half way between Aúlíl and Jermah; the correction, in this case, amounting to only a twenty-second part of the whole distance between those places.

It would be running into needless digression to point out all the contradictions in which El Idrísí involves himself by reducing distances so as to fit them to the frame in which he combines his information, or by expanding details so as to distribute them more equally. It will be here sufficient to have shown that he learned the course of the Great River from El Bekrí, yet that he did not copy his author faithfully, but took liberties with him, which are rendered more conspicuous by the incongruities into which they lead him. He contracts the Desert, spreads out the River; makes Silla on one side only sixteen days distant from the Ocean, and Kúghah, near Seghmárah, on the other, only a month from Dongolah. He wholly misunderstands the account of the lower portion of the river, and by turning the stream westward, he falls into glaring inconsistencies. In conclusion, whatever is reasonable in El Idrísí's account of Ghánah and its vicinity, is taken from El Bekrí, and nearly all of it which is not taken from El Bekrí is absurd. Nevertheless, his statements, when carefully analysed and freed from misconceptions, plainly indicate that Ghánah was situate near that part of the Great River where Tomboktú now stands.[92]

The only novelty worth notice in El Idrísí's account of Western Negroland, is his statement respecting the river of Ghánah, which he informs us was navigable in large boats, and flowed into the ocean. Its mouth was one day's sail from Aúlíl. The river flowing into the ocean near the Bay of Arguin, where it has been shown that the isle and salt mine of Aúlíl were situate, is obviously the Senegal. The short distance of one day's sail, allowed by the Arab geographer in this case, is in just proportion with all his other measures affecting the area of his map.[93] He supposed the Nile of Ghánah, or Great River of the Interior, to unite with the Senegal, and to run westwards into the ocean. Nor is there any rashness in ascribing to him so great a misconception. Leo Africanus makes a precisely similar statement respecting the river of Tomboktú. Having navigated that river from Tomboktú to Jenni, the latter author affirms most positively that it flows westward to the ocean. The only excuse that can be offered for Leo's mistake is, that the part of the river

---

[92] The map of El Idrísí does not represent the conceptions explained above. It makes the Great River divide at Tírka into two branches, so as to form a great island, which he names Wangárah. On the southern branch he places Ghúntil and Ghaïárú, the latter place being 75 days, or 2½ months from Aúlíl, measuring along the river, while only 3½ months at the utmost are allowed for the whole breadth of the continent. El Idrísí writes sometimes in conformity with one of these systems, sometimes with the other. He appears, on examination, to be an unsound author, who, with good materials before him, often wrote without understanding them.

[93] The distance of Aúlíl (in the Bay of Arguin) from Sijilmésah, as stated by El Idrísí, supposes, as we have seen, a mean daily journey of 22½ geographical miles, instead of 15, which is the ordinary rate. Now, if the forty hours' sail from Arguin to the mouth of the Senegal, be reduced in the ratio of 22½ to 15, or 3 to 2, we shall have 26⅔ for the number of hours, according to El Idrísí's scale. But there is no need of such exactness. It is highly improbable that the navigation spoken of by the Arab author, and which formed an ornament of his theory, had any existence even so far as it was within the limits of possibility.

with which he was practically acquainted, has little current, and shows no diminution of magnitude as it is ascended; to a careless observer, therefore, it presents nothing capable of controlling speculation, or guiding to a correct inference respecting the course of the stream. Higher up, the hypothesis was less tenable, and so Melli was placed on a branch of the river. Being biassed by the early Arab writers, particularly El Idrísí, Leo zealously adopted their erroneous opinion, which being repeated by De Barros and other writers on African geography, continued in vogue till the middle of the last century, or nearly six centuries after it was first promulgated.[94] El Idrísí states that salt was carried from Aúlíl to the mouth of the Nile, one day distant, and then up that stream to Silla, Ghánah and Kúghah. Modern authorities, on the other hand, have reported the Senegal to be navigable up to Jenni (two days from Silla), Tomboktú and Gago, at which point their information always terminated. And herein is another point of resemblance between Ghánah and Tomboktú; inasmuch as they hold similar positions in the hypothetical system, connecting the Senegal with the Great River of the Interior.[95]

---

[94] Labat (Ethiop. Occid. 1728, tom. II. p. 125) describes the course of the Niger or Senegal from the lake of Bornú to the sea. Moore (Travels in the Inland Parts of Africa, 1738) also maintained that the Senegal (of which the Gambia was supposed to be a branch) is the Niger, although he at the same time published the Journal of Capt. Stibbs, who was adverse to that opinion. An earlier writer tells us that "the English were frustrated in their attempts to ascend the Niger to the gold countries of Gago, by the osiers among other things." (Charant, Réponses à diverses questions, &c. appended to Frejus, Voyage dans la Mauritanie, 1666.)

[95] El Idrísí says (Rec. de Voy. p. 11) that the salt of Aúlíl was carried up the river to Silla, Tekrúr, Berísa, Ghánah, Kúghah, and the other countries of the blacks. Let it be observed, that while propounding the hypothesis of a navigable river extending across Africa from the Western Ocean to Bornú, the Arab author knew nothing of its navigated course except between Silla and Kúghah or Kághó; that is to say, the generally navigated part of the river of Ghánah, which was evidently identical with that of the river of Tomboktú. The information of our early travellers respecting the Great River of the interior always terminated at Gago. This form of the name was taken from Leo; but Cadamosto had written Cochia (Kúghah), which was probably borrowed from the Mandingoes.

The Western Desert is represented by El Idrísí with the changed aspect consequent on the movement of the Morabites. The Lumtúnah had gone northwards to Morocco, and the Benú Goddálah, to whatever quarter they had migrated, were no longer predominant in the south-western portion of the Ṣaḥrá. The inhospitable tract extending between the desert of Tíser and the Ocean, is named by El Idrísí Kamnúdíyah, the chief town of which was half way between Silla and Arkí. South of Kamnúdíyah, he places a country, the name of which, vitiated by copyists, occurs under a great variety of forms, as, for example, Maghráwah, Meghrárah, Meghzárah, &c. Of these readings, the first alone admits of a satisfactory explanation, and shall therefore be here adopted.[96] Maghráwah lay to the west of Ghánah, and as it extended from Aúlíl, on the sea shore, to Silla and Tekrúr inclusively, it also embraced a territory lying to the south of that State.[97] The country named by El Idrísí Maghráwah is therefore obviously the same which a century earlier had been occupied by the Benú Goddálah, and the change of its name may be naturally ascribed to the revolution which carried away the latter people with the hordes of the Morabites. The Arab historians are silent with respect to those who took the place of the Benú Goddálah; but the want of information may be in this instance supplied by a very probable conjecture.

When the Morabites, having subjugated Sús, Daráh, Sijilmésah, and the province wherein they afterwards founded

[96] To the usual various readings, Meghzárah, Meghrárah, Meghwárah, Mekzárah, &c., M. De Humboldt (Histoire de Géographie, I. p. 291) has added Mufráda. D'Herbelot (under the title Maczarat) seems to consider this to be the name of a fortress, and not of an extensive region. In the Rec. de Voy. v. this name, where it first occurs (p. 10), is written Maghráwah مغراوة (afterwards changed into Maghzárah مغزارة); and the copy of Ibn el Wardi, in the possession of D. P. de Gayangos, has Maghráwah throughout.

[97] Rec. de Voy. v. pp. 10, 13, 18. In the first of the passages here cited, Maghráwah is represented as extending from Aúlíl to the Great River, and including also those countries which the author, by misconstruction of El Bekrí's statements, brought into the vicinity of that part of the river. It is to be lamented that the Translation of El Idrísí's Geography, published in the Rec. de Voy. swarms with false readings, against which little care has been taken to guard the reader.

Morocco, still continued to press northwards, they met with a vigorous resistance from the Maghráwah, who had long ruled over Fez and its dependencies, and who now united with the Miknésah and other Zenátah tribes to oppose the invaders.[98] The victory fell to the Morabites, who entered Fez in triumph in A.D. 1067. But, grown negligent through continual success, they were soon after taken by surprise, overpowered, and expelled. Their enthusiasm, however, was not to be subdued by slight reverses; they returned to the struggle, and again entered Fez in 1069, slaughtering, it is said, 20,000 of the Maghráwah, whose sway in the west thus terminated, after a continuance of just a century.[99]

Of the fortunes of the defeated tribes, there is nothing recorded; but the general tenor of the history of Barbary justifies the supposition that they betook themselves to the desert.[100] In 1084, Yúsef ben Táshifín, the Amír or chief of the Morabites, sent messengers into the Ṣaḥrá, to the Lumtúnah, Goddálah, and Masúfah, announcing to them that he possessed extensive territories, well watered, which he was

---

[98] The Maghráwah مغراوة rose into importance about A.D. 945 (Marmol, I. fol. 127). Their name is written, by Leo Africanus, Magraoa; by Marmol, Magaraoa, or Magaraúa; by Moura (Historia dos Soberanos Mohametanos, &c. Lisbon, 1828) Magraua; and by Conde (Historia de la Dominacion de los Arabes, &c. Madrid, 1820) Magaraba and Magarava. Their original seat, according to Ibn Khaldún, was on the western side of the province of Afrikíah. They are evidently the Machurebii (Μαχυρήβιοι) of Ptolemy, who places them on the right bank of the Chinalaph or Shelíf, near Julia Cæsarea or Shershel, where Dr. Shaw (Travels, I. p. 56) still found an encampment of them; and also on the northern side of the Daradus, the modern Wádi Daráh. El Idrísí, in giving their name to a country, only took the same liberty with it as with those of the Merásah, Seghmárah, &c. which he has converted into the names of towns. The appellation Maghráwaṯ es-Súdán, or of the Blacks, clearly intimates that there was another Maghráwah not on the borders of Negroland. To the scanty account of Maghráwaṯ es-Súdán given by El Idrísí, nothing has been added by later Arab writers save their mistakes.

[99] Moura, Hist. dos Soberanos Moham. p. 121.

[100] The Miknésah, with whom the Maghráwah were associated in their misfortunes, had formerly inhabited the Ṣaḥra, whither they returned in their adversity (Marmol, I. 95; Conde, Dom. de los Arab. I. 411).

ready to bestow on the first comers; "and in a few days," says the historian, "the whole land of Maghreb [Western Barbary and Morocco] was filled with colonists from the Lumtúnah and the other tribes of the desert."[101] It is manifest that the Maghráwah, and their adherents, must have deserted the fine country around Fez, before the half-wild tribes of the Ṣaḥrá were called in to occupy it; and it is probable that, in the course of revolution, they stepped into the place of the Benú Goddálah soon after the latter had accepted the invitation sent to them to fill the vacancy left by the expelled tribes. Thus we are led to conclude, that the territory of the Benú Goddálah passed into the possession of the Maghráwah at a period subsequent to, and probably not far removed from, the year 1084.

The natural and probable supposition, that the tribes expelled from Mauritania by the Morabites changed places with the latter, and fixed themselves in the desert at the same time that their conquerors rushed into the occupation of the cultivated country, explains at once the great difference between the accounts given of the Western Desert by two authors, one of whom wrote seventeen years before the migration referred to, and the other sixty-nine years after that event. Nevertheless, the desire inherent in the human mind to give importance to whatever is obscure, favoured by the corruption of the name Maghráwah, and the garbled accounts of the country so designated, may revolt against a conjecture which confines that name to the Desert, instead of extending it over a large tract of Negroland. Yet El Idrísí plainly states that Maghráwah was a desert; that it was bounded on the north by the middle tract of the Ṣaḥrá, named Kamnúdíyah; and that it extended from Aúlíl, which was its capital, to Silla and Tekrúr; so that it must have been on the northern side of the Great River, of which the Senegal, according to his system, was a part.[2] The same writer indeed includes Silla and

---

[101] Conde, II. pp. 99, 100.

[2] After naming the towns of Maghráwah, he adds (Rec. de Voy. p. 11) that the rest of the country bordering on the river is a sandy desert; and again, he says (p. 107) that the country between Kamnúdíyah and the river, that is, Maghráwah,

Tekrúr in Maghráwah, whence it may be inferred that the exiles from Fez soon obtained the ascendancy due to superior civilization, and became the rulers of their black neighbours. But since the Arabs nowhere mention the Mandingoes, Serakholies, Fúlahs, Wolofs, or other black nations between Silla and the ocean, it must be presumed that they had no direct intercourse with that part of Negroland, and knew nothing of it; and, besides, it is unreasonable to suppose that they described the country south of the Senegal under the general name of Maghráwah, of which general name, in any shape, not the least trace now remains in the region to which it is supposed to have been applied. North of the river, on the other hand, the disappearance of a particular tribe, or of its name; or a loss on the part of any tribe of that predominance which determines the name of a territory, is much more explicable. And if it be admitted that the name Aúlíl or Aúlílí was derived from that of Walílí, the chief place of the Maghráwah and the capital of Western Barbary under their dominion, then the presumption will arise, that some of that nation were always mingled with the Goddálah, and carried the local name to which they were attached, from the shores of the Mediterranean to those of the Ṣaḥrá.[103]

---

is all desert. Hence Ibn el Wardi (Not. et Extr. II. 35) describes Maghráwah as an unfrequented and uninhabitable region. The same writer also observes, in a passage not translated by M. De Guisnes, that Maghráwah is the same country as Maghrebu-l-akṣa, or the Extreme West, a name certainly not applied to Negroland.

[103] Tanjah or Tangiers was anciently called Walílí. Another place of the same name, and of much celebrity, was situate near Fez. Let it be observed, that the name read in the text Aúlílí, may be also read A'walílí; and that there is some reason to suspect that nouns of race or nation are formed by prefixing aleph.

MALI.—The Extinction of Ghánah.

THE catastrophe which caused the disappearance of Ghánah from the political horizon of Negroland, is not distinctly described by any of the Arab historians. Nevertheless, so much light is thrown on the circumstances attending the extinction of that kingdom, in Ibn Khaldún's sketch of the history of Málí, as may enable us to trace the course of those early events with tolerable precision. The statements of that valuable author shall be here given in his own words[104]:—

"When the conquest of the West (by the Arabs) was completed, and merchants began to penetrate into the interior, they saw no nation of the Blacks so mighty as Ghánah, the dominions of which extended westward as far as the Ocean. The King's court was kept in the city of Ghánah, which, according to the author of the Book of Roger (El Idrísí), and the author of the Book of Roads and Realms (El Bekrí), is divided into two parts, standing on both banks of the Nile, and ranks among the largest and most populous cities of the world.[5]

"The people of Ghánah had for neighbours, on the east, a nation, which, according to historians, was called Ṣúṣú; after which came another named Málí; and after that another known by the name of Kaúkaú; although some people prefer a different orthography, and write this name Kághó. The last-named nation was followed by a people called Tekrúr.[6]

---

[104] This extract is taken from Ibn Khaldún's Prolegomena, contained in the first volume of his 'General History of the Arabs and Berbers,' of which volume the library of the British Museum possesses a copy. (MS. B.M. No. 9,574, fol. 90 v.) A few passages here omitted, will be discussed elsewhere.

[5] This is manifestly a mistake. El Bekrí did not, though El Idrísí did, give such a description of Ghánah. But the positive statement preponderated. The Arabs were not critical enough to weigh negative against affirmative evidence.

[6] Ṣúṣú صوصو, or Súsú سوسو — Málí مالي — Kaúkaú كوكو ; Kághó كاغو. The expression *east* must be here understood to mean towards the interior, or *south*. The Arab geographers in general had no idea of Negroland west of Ghánah, and very inadequate conceptions of its extent southwards.

The people of Ghánah declined in course of time, being overwhelmed or absorbed by the Molaththemún (or muffled people —that is, the Morabites), who, adjoining them on the north towards the Berber country, attacked them, and, taking possession of their territory, compelled them to embrace the Mohammedan religion.[107] The people of Ghánah, being invaded at a later period by the Ṣúṣú, a nation of Blacks in their neighbourhood, were exterminated, or mixed with other Black nations.

" As to the people of Málí, they surpassed the other Blacks in those countries in wealth and numbers. They extended their dominions, and conquered the Ṣúṣú, as well as the kingdom of Ghánah in the vicinity of the Ocean towards the west. The Mohammedans say, that the first King of Málí was Baramindánah. He performed the pilgrimage to Mekkah, and enjoined his successors to do the same.[8]

" But the great King of Málí who conquered the Ṣúṣú, and took their country, was named Mári Jáṭah, which means, in the language of that country, Amír Lion, for ***Mári*** signifies an Amír, or prince of the blood royal, and ***jáṭah*** means a lion. These people also style the relatives and connexions of the royal family ***Tikin***.[9] We were not able to learn anything

---

[107] The tribes of the Desert in general, Tawárik, Zenágah, &c. cover the lower part of the face with a muffle or wrapper called *lithám*. They consider it an impropriety to let the mouth be seen. From wearing the lithám they are named Molaththemún, or Muffled. The invasion of Ghánah by the Berbers, alluded to in the text, took place in the year of the Hijra 469.

[8] Baramindánah بَرمَنذَانَة. " Thus the name was spelt (says Ibn Khaldún) by the Sheikh 'Othmán, a doctor and theologian of the people of Ghánah (Ahli Ghánah), and one of the chief men of that country, whom I met in Egypt in 796," &c.

[9] Mári Jáṭah جاطة ماري — Tikin تكن. These words belong to the Mandingo language. *Mari*, master, is found in the Rev. R. M. M'Brair's Grammar of the Mandingo, p. 40 ; *jatto*, a lion, p. 42. In Moore's vocabulary, (in Astley's Collection, II. p. 294,) this word is written *jatta*. The obscure and frequently nasal sound of the final vowels, seems common to both the Súsú and Mandingo languages. The title *Tiguing* occurs in Isaaco's Journal (Park's Second Journey) ; and in Tomboktú according to Caillié's vocabulary (III. p. 313), the word *Tigini* signifies *King*.

further respecting this king, and cannot therefore give his genealogy. Nevertheless I was informed that he reigned five and twenty years.

"He was succeeded by his son Mansá Walí—that is, Sultan 'Alí—who was one of the greatest kings that ever reigned over the people of Málí. He performed the pilgrimage to Mekkah in the reign of the Sultan Ez̤-Z̤áhir Bíbárs.[10] To him succeeded his brother Walí; after whom came another brother, named Khalífah, who was insane, and amused himself with shooting arrows at his subjects. They rushed on him one day and killed him.

"After him came Abú Bekr, who was descended from Mári Jáṭah in the female line. The people of Málí, following in this respect the custom of the 'Ajem (strangers), among whom the sisters and sisters' sons succeed to the inheritance, chose him for their king. We have not been able to learn his lineage, nor the origin of his father.

"Abú Bekr was followed by a freedman named Sákúrah, who usurped the throne.[11] This king made the pilgrimage to Mekkah, during the reign of Almalik Annáṣir; but on his return was killed at Tájúrá. The empire was increased, under him, by the subjugation of other Black nations. It was in his time that the people of Málí made the conquest of Kaúkaú, and added it to their dominions, which already extended from the Ocean and Ghánah in the west, to the country of Tekrúr in the east. Some, however, maintain that the conquest of Kaúkaú was made later. Hájí Túnis, interpreter of Tekrúr, says that the conquest of Kaúkaú was achieved by a general of Mansá Músa, whose name was Saghminḥuh.

"After Sákúrah the kingdom reverted to the posterity of Mári Jáṭah, and Mansá Músa, son of Abú Bekr, ascended the throne. He was an excellent prince, and performed the pil-

---

10 Mansá Wali منسا ولي. Mansá, king, is found in all the Mandingo vocabularies. Changed into Manso, and taking a nasal termination, it becomes Mansong. The name here read Wali is evidently the Woolli so frequently occurring in the modern accounts of Tomboktú and the country of the Mandingoes.

11 Sákúrah سَاكُورَة.

grimage in 724.. The number of people employed to carry his baggage and provisions amounted to 12,000, all dressed in tunics of figured cotton, or the silk called El-Yemení. The Hájí Túnis, interpreter of this nation in Káhirah (Cairo), said that Mansá Músa brought with him to Egypt no less than 80 loads of Tibar (gold dust), each weighing 300 pounds. He brought the whole on camels, though in his own kingdom camels are not used, baggage being there carried on the backs of slaves.[112] Mansá Músa, on his return, conceived the idea of building himself a fine palace. Abú Iṣḥaḳ showed him a model, and erected the edifice, with plaster and all kinds of ornaments, for which he received 12,000 mithḳáls of gold. Mansá Músa maintained an intimate and friendly correspondence with Sultan Abú-l-Ḥasan, of Al-Maghreb, and reigned twenty-five years.

" On his death the empire devolved on Mansá Maghá—that is, Sultan Mohammed, for in their language Maghá signifies Mohammed. He died after a reign of four years, and was succeeded by Mansá Suleïmán, son of Abú Bekr, and brother of Musá, who reigned twenty-four years. After him came his son, Mansá Ibn Suleïmán, who died nine months after ascending the throne. Then followed Mári Jáṭah, and Mansá Maghá, son of Mansá Músa, and reigned fourteen years. He (Mári Jáṭah) was a wicked and dissolute prince. He sent an embassy to Abú Selím, son of Abú-l-Ḥasan, Sultan of Al-Maghreb (the West), which embassy arrived in Fez in the year 762; and among other presents which came with it, were some very tall animals called Zeráfah (camelopards), as high as obelisks, and strange in the land of Al-Maghreb.

" Abú Abdullah Mohammed Ibn Wásúl, a native of Sijilmésah, and who inhabited for a long time the city of Kaúkaú, in their country (*i. e.* in the empire of Málí), where he performed the duties of Cadhi, told me, when I met him in 776, much more respecting the kings of that country than I can

---

[112] Mansá Músa منسا موسي is styled the King of Tekrúr by Makrízí, who relates his visit to Egypt on his way to Mekkah, and describes the wealth and pompous retinue of the Negro king, in language to which even that author's great reputation will hardly secure implicit credit. See Not. et Extr. tom. XII. p. 637.

relate. He said that this Sultan Jáṭah was the worst king that ever existed; that he wasted the treasures, was on the point of destroying the palace erected by his ancestors; and that he even sold to certain Egyptian merchants, for a trifling sum of money, a huge mass of native gold, weighing 20 cwt., and preserved among other curiosities in the royal treasure. Providence, however, punished him; for he was afflicted with a disease very common in those countries, and the ravages of which are particularly frequent among the higher classes. It begins with a kind of lethargy or stupor, which renders the sufferer insensible during the greater part of the day. After lingering two years under this incurable malady, Jáṭah died in 775.[13]

"The people of Málí chose his son Músa to succeed him. He was a just prince, but was overpowered by his wazír Mári Jáṭah, who threw him into confinement, and usurped all the powers of sovereignty. This Wazír has made some conquests towards the east. Passing the limits of Kaúkaú, he arrived at the stations or fixed habitations in the land of Tekaddá, which is behind the country of the Morabites; but he has since restored that territory to its own Sultan. Tekaddá is seventy days from Wergelán towards the south-west; the road of the pilgrims (from Kaúkaú to Egypt) passes through it. Sultan Músa is on friendly terms with the rulers of Záb and Wergelán."[14]

---

[13] It is surprising that a historian of so much sense as Ibn Khaldún should join in censuring King Jáṭah for the imaginary offence of selling a mass of gold of a ton weight. The fable of a large mass of gold in the royal treasure first referred to Ghánah (Not. et Extr. p. 645), then to Málí, and lastly to Tomboktú; where, however, the precious lump was reduced to the weight of 1,300 lb. (Leo, pt. VII. c. 5.) Winterbottom (Account of the Native Africans at Sierra Leone, II. p. 29), a competent medical authority, describes the disease above alluded to, which, he says, proves fatal in every instance. "The disposition to sleep is so strong as scarcely to leave a sufficient respite for the taking of food. Even the repeated application of the whip, a remedy which has been frequently used, is hardly sufficient to keep the poor wretch awake."

[14] Tekaddá تكدا — Az-záb الزاب. This is the country of the Mezzábí, north-west of Wergelán.

Ibn Khaldún further relates, that, after having written the preceding historical sketch, he learned that Mansá Músa died in 789, and was succeeded by his brother Mansá Maghá. He being killed a year after, the vacant throne was seized by Ṣanadaki, who had married Músa's mother, and whose name means Wazír.[115] But this usurper was deposed in a few months by a descendant of Mári Jáṭah. A prince named Maḥmúd, who came from the country of the Infidels in the interior, and who was descended from Mansá Kú, son of Mansá Walí, son of Mári Jáṭah the First, was king of Málí in A.H. 792.

It is stated in the foregoing extract that Ghánah merged in the empire of the Morabites, an event which may be assigned, with much probability, to the year of the Hijra 469, when the Mohammedan faith was forcibly imposed on the pagan nations of Negroland contiguous to the Western Desert.[16] But the Morabites, bred up in a wild life, and under a loose patriarchal authority, cannot be supposed to have thought much of social or political organization. It is likely that they extended their dominions without propagating a form of government, and that the kingdom of Ghánah remained little changed by the loss of its independence. In the time of El Idrísí, or a little before the year of the Hijra 548, it was ruled by a descendant of Abú Táleb—that is, by a Zenágah—and this state of things continued probably half a century longer.[17]

But towards the interior, or south from Ghánah, were the following nations, viz.:—the Ṣúṣú, Málí, Kaúkaú or Kághó, and Tekrúr. In arranging these nations all eastward from

---

115 Sanadaki probably means High or Supreme Counsellor, from *san* or *sanon*, high, and *adégué*, a counsellor. (Dard's Dict.) Jarric (Hist. des Choses Mémorables, III. p. 372) pleasantly describes the mode of dubbing a *Solatequi* among the Zapes (now called *Bullom*, or lowlanders), near Sierra Leone. In Isaaco's Journal (Park's Second Journey, 8vo. p. 238), mention is made of a king styled *Sallatigua*-Koura. From this word is evidently derived the title *Seratik*, borne by the King in Bambúk and some of the Fellátah states.

16 Not. et Extr. p. 642, note. Marmol, III. fol. 21. Abú Bekr ben Omar was the Morabite conqueror of Negroland, whither he retired after the rise of Yúsef ben Táshifín. Moura, Hist. dos Soberanos, &c., p. 146.

17 "The Zenágah," says Ibn Khaldún (fol. 68 v), "claim to stand in the same relationship to Abú Táleb, as do the Maghráwah to 'Othmán ben 'Afan."

Ghánah, Ibn Khaldún showed a very imperfect conception of the geography of Negroland, and particularly of its comparative geography. Though the name Tekrúr may have belonged in his time to a country beyond Kághó, or south-eastwards from Ghánah, yet it certainly designated a kingdom south-westwards from that capital in the period anterior to the rise of Málí. The Ṣúṣú at present occupy a maritime district comprising the basin of the river Scarcies, wherein they have been established at least three centuries. Their language would favour the supposition that they are remotely connected with the Mandingoes. The people of Málí were certainly of the latter race; and it is probable that they and the Ṣúṣú were kindred tribes, who, like the Manes and Mosí of later times, issued from the interior; or—if for the sake of preciseness we may in this instance hazard a conjecture—from the country lying between Kong, Bergú, Ghúrma, and Dahómy.[18] The precise dates of the invasion of Ghánah by the Ṣúṣú and the people of Málí are not given by Ibn Khaldún. We are informed, however, that Mansá Suleïmán, a prince bearing a Mandingo title, founded Tomboktú in A.H. 610; and since he is not included in the list of the kings of Málí, we are warranted in considering him a king of the Ṣúṣú, whose conquest of Ghánah must therefore have taken place between the years 548 and 610 of the Hijra, probably not long anterior to the latter date.

---

[18] The Mandingo and Ṣúṣú languages at present differ widely from each other, but many circumstances, nevertheless, combine to prove the ancient affinity of the two nations. They are so frequently confounded together, that it is not easy to discover the limits of the Ṣúṣú country. Rennell, writing from Major Houghton's information (Elucidations, &c. in Proc. Afr. Assoc. I. 275), calls "Mandinga, the country of the Susos." Adanson (Voy. au Senegal, 1757, p. 89), after stating that the people dwelling on the banks of the Gambia are Mandingoes, adds, "ou Sosés, pour m'exprimer comme eux." The Ṣúṣú language, which is widely understood, is most correctly spoken by the Mandingoes (Gram. and Vocab. of the Susoo Language, 1802, p. 48). The Jesuit missionaries unite the two nations; "Zozoes, casta de Mandingos," says Sandoval (Hist. de Ethiop. p. 43; see also Jarric, Hist. des Choses Mémor. III. p. 411). Winterbottom (Account of Nations at Sierra Leone, I. p. 5,) extends the Ṣúṣú country from the River Kissee to the Rio Nuñez.

From the dynasty of the Ṣúṣú, then, dates the importance of Tomboktú:[119] but their empire did not continue long. The reign of Mári Jáṭah, the conqueror of the Ṣúṣu, probably commenced about the year 630; and with the kings of Málí begins a connected historical record.

It is worthy of observation, that the conquests here related proceeded in the direction of wealth and commerce, and stopped where these allurements terminated. Ghánah and Tomboktú appear to have remained for a long time the furthest bounds of the empire of Málí. Eighty years elapsed before Kághó was annexed to that empire; and as many more before the passion for conquest led Ṣanadaki to invade Tekaddá, a worthless possession, which was soon abandoned. Thus the Great River formed for many hundred miles the boundary of the empire of Málí, that is, of the Mandingoes, who are still extensively spread over the same ample region, and who chiefly uphold its trade, industry, and civilization. It is evident that Ghánah, conquered by the Ṣúṣú, the founders of Tomboktú, and annexed to Málí eighty years before this empire extended to Kághó, was the frontier of Negroland facing Sijilmésah, and consequently the tract wherein Tomboktú now stands. Nor is it difficult to explain why the kingdom of Ghánah disappeared from the political horizon in the course of these events; for the conquerors had, with a new language, a form of government capable of absorbing all foreign and inferior titles, and of establishing its own in their stead. The title GHANAH, therefore, was superseded by that of MANSA.—The principal events recorded in the history of Ghánah, and the succession of the Kings of Málí, shall be here repeated in a tabular form, and arranged chronologically; the date subjoined to each reign being, as far as can be ascertained, that of its commencement.

---

119 Leo says (pt. VII. c. 5) that Tomboktú was built by Mansá Suleïmán, but yet there is reason to suspect that he only improved and raised into importance a place previously existing. Conde (Hist. de la Dominacion, &c., I. p. 402,) speaks of a chieftain named Mansur el Tombuzi; but this title is probably a misreading for Tombúṭí; Tomboktú being commonly called in Barbary Tombúṭ, or Tombúṭo. The passage here referred to occurs in the annals of the year 297 H. (A.D. 909.)

		A.H.	A.D.
GHANAH	(properly the King's title) deprived of Aúdaghost in	446	1054
	Still independent in	460	1067
	Compelled by the Morabites to relinquish Idolatry and embrace the Mohammedan faith	469	1076
	Ruled by a descendant of Abú Táleb (i. e. one of the Zenágah nation)	548	1153
ṢUṢU.	Ghánah conquered by the Ṣúṣú.		
	Tomboktú founded by Mansá Suleïmán	610	1213
	N.B.—The title Ghánah superseded by that of Mansá.		
MALI.	Mári Jáṭah conquered the Ṣúṣú, and reigned 25 years.		
	Mansá Walí (son of the preceding) performed the pilgrimage to Mekkah in the reign of Bibárs	658–75	1259–76
	Mansá Walí (brother of the preceding).		
	Mansá Khalífah (another brother).		
	Mansá Abú Bekr (descended from Mári Jáṭah in the female line).		
	Sákúrah, a usurper, went to Mekkah in the time of Almalik An-Nasír, and therefore subsequent to	710	1310
	(The conquest of Kaúkaú is ascribed by some to the reign of Sákúrah, by others to that which follows.)		
	Mansá Músa (son of Abú Bekr) performed the pilgrimage in	724	1324
	Mansá Maghá (son of the preceding) reigned 4 years	732	1331–2
	Mansá Suleïmán (son of Abú Bekr) reigned 24 years	736	1335–6
	He was visited by Ibn Baṭúṭah in	753	1352
	Mansá Ibn Suleïmán (son of the preceding) reigned 9 months	760	1359
	Mansá Jáṭah (son of Mansá Maghá) ascended the throne in	761	1360
	and reigned 14 years.		
	Mansá Músa (son of the preceding) reigned 14 years	775	1373
	His Wazír, Mári Jáṭah, usurped the sovereign power, and conquered Tekaddá, which was soon after relinquished.		
	Mansá Maghá (brother of the preceding)	789	1387
	Ṣanadaki, (i. e. the Wazír) and another usurper.		
	Maḥmúd, a descendant of Mári Jáṭah the first, was king of Málí in	792	1390

The position of all the places mentioned in the preceding historical sketch, may be satisfactorily ascertained from the narrative of Ibn Baṭúṭah, who visited Negroland about half a century earlier than the date of Ibn Khaldún's history, and whose remarks throw a valuable light on the geography and social condition of the countries then known under that denomination. A succinct account, therefore, of his journey into Negroland shall be here given, for the sake of the elucidations derivable from it.

IBN BAṬÚṬAH'S JOURNEY.

POSITION OF MALI.

Ibn Baṭúṭah returned to his native city in 1350, after an absence of five and twenty years, during which time he had visited nearly all the countries of the east, from Constantinople to China, from Bulghar and Kipchak Tatary to Zingebar and the Indian islands. He employed the next year in visiting Spain and Barbary; and then, to complete his acquaintance with the habitable earth, he undertook the perilous journey over the desert to the country of the Blacks.[120] In Sijilmésah he was hospitably entertained by the brother of a merchant whom he had met at Kan-chan-fu in China, and, purchasing camels and provisions for four months, he joined a Káfilah which set forward on its march to Negroland on the 1st of February 1352, under the guidance of Abú Mohammed Bandakán, of the tribe of Masúfah.

---

[120] For an account of Ibn Baṭúṭah, whose Travels at least equal in interest those of Marco Polo, see the 'History of the Mohammedan Dynasties in Spain,' by D. Pascual de Gayangos, p. 348. This gentleman possesses a copy of the complete narrative of Ibn Baṭúṭah, and from his translation of it (which we hope will be presented to the public ere long) have been collected the passages given above, which are not in general to be found in Professor Lee's translation of the abridgment of the same work.

In twenty-five days the Káfilah arrived at Tegháza, a town in the desert, where the houses were built of rock salt, and roofed with camel skins. The inhabitants of the place were slaves of the Masúfah, employed in excavating and cutting the salt required for the trade with Negroland. After a delay of ten days on the hill near Tegháza, and renewing its stock of water at the salt and muddy wells in the hollow (the supply for the next ten days in the desert being precarious), the Káfilah resumed its march.[21] It fortunately escaped the much dreaded difficulties: fresh rain-water lay in all the hollows and crevices of the rocks; and at one place was found

---

[21] Tegháza تَغَازِي is described, though not named, by El Bekrí (Not. et Extr. p. 436). The salt mines, he says, are two days from the Great Desert, over which passes the road to Ghánah, and twenty from Sijilmésah. Ibn Baṭúṭah, travelling slowly, found the latter distance to be a journey of twenty-five days. The Morabite general, Abú Bekr ben Omar, purchased Negro slaves at a place in the desert called Gasza, whom he sent to Spain, and exchanged for European slaves, to recruit his army (Conde, Hist. de la Dom. II. p. 86). The Gasza here mentioned is probably Tegháza mutilated in the original text, and further disfigured by the Spanish writer. El Idrísí (Rec. de Voy. p. 107) mentions a place in the desert called Taghíza. According to Cadamosto (c. XII. fol. 137 v), Tegháza signifies *Cargadore*, or a loader (an old word, ill changed into *Caricatojo* in the recent edition of Ramusio); importing that the place so called was the residence of those who loaded the camels, or furnished the freight for the trade with Negroland. Peritsol (Itinera Mundi, ed. by Hyde, p. 124), explains it otherwise, and translates Tegháza, *earth* loaded *with gold*. Ibn Baṭúṭah says, that at Aïwalátin the salt fetched from ten to eighteen mithḳáls the load, and at Málí twenty or thirty, or sometimes forty mithḳáls; and Leo states that when he was at Tomboktú, the price of a load of salt rose there to eighty ducats. Cadamosto quotes much higher prices. The ducat or mithḳál is valued by Jackson at 3*s*. 8*d*. Another writer informs us, that the load of salt (600 lb.), worth 4*s*. at Tegháza, paid 5*l*. duty at Gago (True Historical Discourse of Muley Hamet's Rising, c. II.). It has been asserted by Jackson (Account of Morocco, p. 241), and too readily believed, that there is a second Tegháza near the coast. But that author's meaning is explained by his map, in which we find written *East Tarassa* (Tegháza) and *West Tarassa Arabs* (the Trarzas, or, as Labat writes their name, Eteraza). According to Jackson's orthographical system, the same Arabic name may be written Tegháza, Tegrassa, or Terassa. Caillié (Voy. &c. tom. II. p. 417,) came to some wells called Trarzas, or Trasas, within the region of loose sand, and which have been nevertheless mistaken for the site of Tegháza, whereas they obviously owed their name to the tribe that dug them.

so copious a spring of delicious water, that the travellers, after satisfying their thirst, washed themselves and their clothes in the limpid stream. The fine truffles growing in this tract, compensated in some degree for the troublesome insects infesting it. One of the merchants belonging to the Káfilah strayed too far from it, and was lost. This misfortune served as a warning to Ibn Baṭúṭah, who had previously made it a practice to march in advance and wander over the plains. The dead body of the strayed merchant was afterwards found by another Káfilah about a mile from water.

Táserahlá, the station at which the Káfilah next arrived, was a stagnant pool, where it was customary to halt three days, for the purpose of repairing and replenishing the water-skins. It was also usual to send forward from this place the couriers (el takshíf), a name commonly given to all of the tribe of Masúfah.[122] For merchants arriving at Táserahlá always despatched letters to Aïwalátin, apprising their friends of their approach, and engaging them to meet the Káfilah with water four days from the latter place. If the courier died on the way, as often happened, then no assistance came from

---

122 Táserahlá تَاسَرَهلا. Respecting the Masúfah, who were generally called el Takshíf, that is, the scouts or couriers, and who appear to have occupied the whole road from Tegháza to Tomboktú, there is a passage in Ibn Khaldún (fol. 89) which, with a little abridgment, is worth transcribing.—"After the fall of the Morabite dynasty, the tribes of the Molaththemún returned to the desert, and now occupy the countries which they originally possessed in the vicinity of Negroland. But as we have already observed, the emigration of the Zenágah tribes was but partial: a few only of the Masúfah and Lumtúnah obeyed the impulse, while the majority of the tribes remained behind, and *keep in our days their old settlements in the Sahrá*, paying tribute to the Kings of Negroland, on whom they depend, and in whose armies they serve. The Goddálah are directly opposite to the Dhawi-Hassán, a branch of the Moákel Arabs, settled in Sús el Akṣa ; the Lumtúnah are opposite to the Dhawi-Mansúr and Dhawi 'Obeidu-llah, branches of the same great tribe living in Maghrebu-l-Akṣa. The Masúfah face the Zaghabah, an Arab tribe in Maghrebu-l-Aúsat ; and the Lamṭah adjoin the Benú Riyyah, who occupy Ez-Záb."—Thus it appears that the Masúfah inhabiting the tract of desert between Sijilmésah and Tomboktú were in *their old settlements*, and, therefore, in the tract between Sijilmésah and Ghánah. (See page 17.) Leo (pt. I. c. 17–19) points out the situation of the various families of the Machil (Moákel) tribe of Arabs.

Aïwalátin, and the Káfilah perished in consequence. "For," says the Arab author, "that desert is filled with demons; and if the courier goes alone, they forthwith appear, bewilder and startle him, till he strays from the way, when his destruction is inevitable; for there is no path or track to guide him, nor anything but an immense wilderness of sand driven about by the winds, so that where there is now a level plain, there arises in a few minutes a hillock, which again quickly disappears. The guides in this desert, therefore, have nothing to rely on but constant practice, and require no ordinary share of intrepidity and self-possession. The appearance of our guide, who was one of those best acquainted with the country, caused me much surprise, inasmuch as he had but one eye, and that one diseased."[23]

The merchants of the Káfilah engaged a Masúfí courier for 100 mithḳáls of gold, and on the sixth day after leaving Táserahlá, they descried with delight the signal fires of those who had advanced to meet them from Aïwalátin. The tract passed over abounded in herds of the baḳr el wuḥash (the Antelope Bubalis), which were chased by the Masúfah, and killed with arrows. Their flesh, causing thirst, was little eaten: but their stomachs contained water; and Ibn Baṭúṭah saw with astonishment their contents drained by the people of the desert. Serpents were also numerous in the same region. A merchant of Telemsán, who accompanied the Káfilah, amused himself with catching these reptiles; but he was on one occasion bitten in the hand, and the inflammation that ensued continuing to increase, he killed a camel, thrust his wounded hand into the stomach of the slaughtered animal, and kept it there for some hours, till the pain was assuaged. The desert travelled over in the last four days to Aïwalátin differed much from the preceding tract. It was dry and hot in the highest degree. The Káfilah occásionally met with parties of the Masúfah and Berdámah, who carried water about for

---

[23] The solitude and dangers of the desert naturally incline the mind to the terrors of superstition. Marco Polo (Marsden's edit. p. 159) relates that the Desert of Lop, in Tatary, is haunted by spirits who call travellers by their names in the voice of friends, and lead them astray.

sale. In the foregoing account of the desert between Táserahlá and Aïwalátin, it is easy to recognize "The Desert," properly so called, of El Bekrí, the Desert of Tíser of El Idrísí, and the Azawad of Leo. The breadth of the dreaded tract, peopled by the fears of travellers with demons; its distance from Sijilmésah, and from the southern limit of the Ṣaḥrá; its possessors the Masúfah; and the numerous serpents infesting it, are all so many marks whereby it may be discovered under its various denominations.[124]

Two lunar months were spent in the journey from Sijilmésah to Aïwalátin.[25] This was the frontier territory of Málí, and had for ruler a black officer named Ḥuseïn Farbá, the word *farbá* signifying *governor* in the language of Málí.

---

124 A hundred mithḳáls was a large hire, if we estimate it by the price of salt at Tegháza, which was probably but one mithḳál the load. In the descriptions of the Desert of Tíser, the serpents infesting it are always mentioned. They were dressed with salt and wormwood, according to El Idrísí (Rec. de Voy. p. 108), and eaten by the Blacks. If the loose hot sands abruptly approach the limits of vegetation on the southern border of the Ṣaḥrá, between the 4th and 9th westerly meridians, this phenomenon must be ascribed to the prevalence of northerly winds, which drive the sand within the limit of the rains. On the coast the drift of the sand seems to lean towards the north.

25 Aïwalátin ايولاتن is a regular plural, formed from the singular Walet or Waláta. Thus *afíus*, a hand, makes in the plural *aïfásen* (Höst's Marokos, p. 137); *tar*, a foot, makes *itaren*. The Berber names of towns are often in the plural number, comprehending the several villages within the limits of a *Tenzert*, or district. Waláta (Gualata) is described by Leo (pt. VI. c. 60), not as a town, but a territory containing three hamlets (casali) and some scattered habitations. Hence he might with propriety have written *Igualaten*, as he wrote *Iguaden* for Wádán, the Hoden of Cadamosto. The commercial importance once enjoyed by Aïwalátin is agreeably illustrated by an anecdote related in the History of the Mohammedan Dynasties in Spain, p. 302. While Ibn Baṭúṭah was at the court of Málí, he witnessed one day a Masúfí rushing into the presence of the King, and prostrating himself in the manner of a suppliant. When asked who had wronged him, he replied, Manshajú biwalátin منشاجوا بولاتن, which means the Governor or Viceroy of Aïwalátin. Manshajú or Manshagú is obviously derived from Mansá, with the Berber pronunciation; the *b* prefixed to the following word is the sign of the possessive case (Venture on the Berber Language, in the Appendix to Langlés' Translation of Hornemann's Travels, p. 420).

Ibn Baṭúṭah was but little pleased with the manners of the Blacks, among whom he had expected to see more homage paid to men of his complexion. He even thought of returning immediately to Sijilmésah, but his original plans preponderated, and he resolved, at any rate, to explore Negroland. His attention was engaged by the singular character and customs of the Masúfah, who formed the higher class of the inhabitants of Aïwalátin. Though Mohammedans, they had a law of succession resembling that of the pagans of Malabar. Their women, handsome and finely-formed, went unveiled, and conversed with the men on terms of freedom and equality which fully spoke the dissolute manners of the place.[26]

After staying fifty days in Aïwalátin, Ibn Baṭúṭah engaged a Masúfí guide, and, in company with three merchants, set forward for Málí, which was a good twenty-four days' journey distant. In ten days he came to Zághari, a large town inhabited by black traders, and some whites of the Ibádhíyah sect, called Ṣaghanghú. Leaving Zághari, he arrived at Kársekhó, "a city on the bank of the Great River which is the Nile." After describing the downward course of the river in terms which shall be examined further on, the traveller's narrative thus proceeds:—"We marched from Kársekhó and came to the river Ṣanṣarah, which is ten miles from Málí, and it being the custom of the country that no one enters there without asking leave, I wrote to the company of Whites, and to its chief, Moḥammed ben Alfaḳíh Algezúlí, and also to Shemso-d-dín, to engage me a lodging; and so, when I came to the river (Ṣanṣarah), I embarked in a canoe, and without further trouble, arrived at the city of Málí, the residence of the Sultan of Negroland; and, landing near the burial ground, I walked directly to the quarter of the Whites, and found Moḥammed

[26] The title Farbá فربا, borne by the chief officers in the empire of Málí, is originally the same as that of Farma or Farim, usual among the Ṣúṣú and Mandingoes near the coast. Jobson (The Golden Trade, p. 58) distinguishes between the Ferrans (Farims) and Ferambra (the Farinba of Park). Golberry (Fragm. d'un Voy. I. p. 425) observes, that in Bambúk, the power has passed from the Seratik, or nominal king, to the Farims. The same is true of the neighbouring states, which at present hardly acknowledge a paramount authority. For the Masúfí law of succession, see p. 40.

ben Alfaḳíh, who had procured me a lodging opposite to his own house."[127]

Ibn Baṭúṭah fell sick soon after his arrival in the capital of Málí, and two months elapsed before he was able to visit Mansá Suleïmán. Returning on that occasion from the palace, he was followed by those who brought the King's present. They called to him to rise and receive it, while they bore it towards him with an air of much importance. But what was the surprise of the Arab traveller, who expected to receive a handsome garment, or a sum of money, to find the royal gift to consist of only three scraps of bread, some hashed mutton, and a calabash of milk. He subsequently took occasion to reprove Mansá Suleïmán for his want of munificence, and thereupon received from him, as a conciliatory gift, a robe, lodging, an allowance while he remained, with a sum of money at his departure.

But the arrangements of Mansá Suleïmán's court did not betray the sordid disposition imputed to him. They appear to have been conceived in a style of rude pomp and majesty no longer witnessed in the same country. Within the royal palace was an alcove or vaulted chamber communicating with the interior, and having towards the hall of audience three windows covered with silver gratings, and as many more with gratings of gold or silver gilt. Over these gratings hung silk curtains, the drawing of which served to show that the king was seated within. The officers and people then assembled. The Farárí or chief captains, with their archers, spearmen, and musicians, ranged themselves on both sides of the alcove, and on the signal being given, by thrusting a handkerchief of

---

127 Zághari زَاغَرِي. Its inhabitants were called Zangarátah زَنْجَرَاتَة. While the followers of the Ibadhia doctrine were named Ṣaghanghú صَغَنْغُو, orthodox sunnites were called Túri تُورِي. Ibn Baṭúṭah mentions no river on his route from Aïwalátin to Karsekhó كَارْسَخُو, nor does he state the distance, which probably was not great, from this place to the Ṣanṣarah صَنْصَرَة.

Egyptian muslin through the grating of one of the windows, the musicians fell to work with drums, ivory flutes, pipes of cane and calabashes, and made an extraordinary din. Outside the alcove stood Dúghá, the interpreter, and near him a man who carried his words to the king, and brought back the royal answer.[28]

At times the king gave audience in the open air, seated on a platform covered with silk, and called Bámbi. A large silk umbrella, like a canopy, was held over his head, having on the top a golden bird as large as a falcon. He walked slowly on these occasions, surrounded by 300 armed slaves. Two horses and two rams were led forth, among other emblems of royal state. The King's words gave rise to laudatory harangues in the assembly, in the course of which the soldiers signified their approbation by twanging their bows. Whoever spoke to the King, or was addressed by him, stripped himself to the waist, and, throwing himself prostrate, sprinkled dust or clay over his head, and beat the ground with his elbows. The frequent exhibition of this abject humility offended Ibn Baṭúṭah, who also reprobates the custom of allowing the female slaves and young girls, not excepting the King's daughters, to go completely naked, and to appear in that state before the King himself. He censures also the grotesque exhibitions of the poets or mimes, who were called *jolá* (the plural of *jál*).[29] He witnessed the performance of one who

---

[28] The terms Faráriah فرارية and Farári فراري, applied by Ibn Baṭúṭah to the chief officers of Málí, and which he translated Amírs, are respectively the collective and plural of Arabic form, from the word ***Fary***, which in the Bambara language (a dialect of the Mandingo) signifies ***valour*** or ***courage***. From this word comes ***Fariba***, a valiant man (Dard, Dict. Wolofe et Bambara). The Mandingoes form personal nouns with the suffix *ma:* thus from *fanko*, power, comes *fankama*, a powerful man (M'Brair's Gram. of Mandingo, p. 6). Thus it is probable that from the word ***Fary*** is derived the titles Farba, Farma, or Farim, which the conquests of the Mandingo race have spread so widely through Guinea. But the Farims, or Lieutenants, are now superior to the Seratiks, or Kings, and the title of the latter was at one time secondary (see Note 115); so that sovereign titles in Guinea standing on the ruins of preceding titles, are so many monuments of revolution.

[29] It is obvious that the poets here described are the ***Jelli-kês***, or ***singing men***, of the Mandingoes (see Laing's Travels, p. 232). But it must not be supposed that

wore a masquerade dress of feathers, with a wooden head, like that of some bird, and, thus disguised, delivered an extemporaneous harangue before the King. He says nothing of the industry or trade of Málí; yet the length at which he describes the dresses of the courtiers, and his frequent mention of silks and of gold and silver ornaments, show that the Negro city did not impress his mind with the idea of poverty. The King wore a gown of European manufacture.

Among the Mandingoes or other nations in Western Africa, no trace at present exists of the manners of Málí, or of the pompous forms of a great monarchy. But in Yariba and Bergú, on the banks of the Quorra, we find absolute sovereigns, who are approached with the same humiliating ceremonies above described. While the King sits richly clothed, and the musicians strain their efforts, the courtiers strip themselves to the waist, and bow their heads to the dust. In Bergú the King is followed by a troop of naked girls.[130] The idea of

---

by Jál حال, in the (Arabicized) plural Jolá حُلا, Ibn Baṭúṭah meant to represent the word Jelli-ké. He must be understood to say that the Jelli-kés, in Málí, were of the nation called *Jolá*. Park says (Second Journey, 8vo. p. 57) that "those who trade on credit are called *Juli*." But this appears to be a rash and incorrect explanation of the name. The word *julo* signifies *debt* or bondage, but not a *debtor*. The same author, in describing further on (p. 228) the route southward to Bé-dú, mentions several Juli towns, and observes, that "the Julis are people who understand the language of Bœdoo and Miniana, and are employed as brokers," &c. But our difficulties respecting the application of this name are removed by Caillié, who informs us (Voy. à Temboctou, II. pp. 82, 160), that in Bambara the Mandingoes are called *Jaulas*, *Diaulas*, or *Jolas*. It is probable, however, that the name properly belongs to the inhabitants of the country south of Bambara, where Park pointed out the Juli towns. But in the Bambara language *Dhioli* (according to Dard's orthography) means *red;* may not the Jolá, Julis, or Jaulas, therefore, be the people referred to in the document procured from the Governor of Senegal, and published in the Appendix to Adams's Narrative (p. 197), wherein Bé-dú is described to be "un pays habité par un peuple *rougeatre*"?

130 Clapperton's Second Journey, pp. 47, 52, 72. The persons prostrating themselves before the King of Yariba were contemptuously called "Sandeaters," by Clapperton's Houssa servant; so little are the usages of Ghánah now known in the neighbourhood of Kanó! Lander (Expedition to the Niger, I. p. 172), describing

royalty as regards both its internal principle and external form, is now in Yariba precisely what it was five centuries ago in Málí; and this remarkable fact may perhaps justify the suspicion that the people of Málí originally issued from the country adjoining Bergú, Yariba, and Dahómy, and wherein there now exists a Mohammedan, and probably a Mandingo state called Magho.[31]

Ibn Baṭúṭah relates his departure from Málí in these words: "I arrived in Málí on the 14th of the month Jumáda-l-awwal, of the year 753 (29th June, 1352), and I left it on the 22nd of Moharrem in the following year (27th February, 1353). I departed in company with a merchant named Abú Bekr Ibn Yakúb, and we took the road to Mímah. I rode on a camel, because horses are so dear in that country that one often costs 100 mithḳáls." From these expressions, combined with those in which he describes his arrival in Málí, it appears evident that he never crossed the Great River, and therefore that the city of Málí must have stood on the northern side of that stream. He came to Kársekhó, situate on the northern bank of the Great River, "which is the Nile." He did not cross this stream, but proceeding to the river Ṣanṣarah, and embarking on it, he reached Málí. When quitting this place, he mounted his camel at once, and took the road to Mímah. It is therefore certain that Málí was on the same bank of the Great River as Kársekhó and Mímah.

---

these ceremonies, names the king Mansolah, of which the Mandingo title Mansá may possibly be a part.

[31] It is manifest that the kingdom called Maha by Clapperton (Second Journey, p. 56) is the Magho of Dupuis (Residence in Ashantee, p. xcviii), and is also identical with the Mohammedan kingdom of Zogho, said by the latter writer (p. civ.) to adjoin the Yagah tribes (Bergú) and the Ayah (Yariba). The road from Ashantee to Niki, the capital of Bergú, after passing through the town of Zogho, conducts to Salamo, Jambodú, and Súsú, or Súso. The last two names are apparently Mandingo. The name of the Sultan of Magho, residing in the city of Ghoroma (Ghúrma) is said (Dupuis, p. cxxix.) to be Mariba Sheky, an obvious misreading for Farba Shego. It seems very likely that the title of Maha or Magho, vaguely given by the people on the coast to a Mohammedan prince in the interior, is the Mandingo name Maghá, that is, Mohammed.

To this conclusion it may be objected, that Leo Africanus places Melli (Málí) on a southern branch of the Great River, or Niger, as he styles it. But that writer's statements, if viewed comprehensively, and thoroughly understood, will be found to afford, in this instance, no firm ground whereon to build an argument. He says that the country called by the Moors Gheneoa (Genéwah), and by the natives Genni (Jenni), extends 250 miles along the Niger, to the place where that river enters the ocean. And again, he says that Melli lies to the south of Gheneoa, and extends 300 miles along a branch of the Niger. Now it is obvious that the river on which Melli stood, is converted into a branch of the Niger by the same hypothesis which led the river of Genni directly westward to the ocean; and we are not bound, while rejecting the erroneous theory, to respect the modifications forced by it on collateral information; nor to admit Leo's descriptions, clothed in the language of system, in opposition to Ibn Baṭúṭah's clear statement of facts.[132]

But if we cannot admit that the capital of Málí was situate on any stream entering the Joliba from the south, so neither can it be supposed to have stood on any tributary stream joining that river on its left or northern bank. For why should a traveller make such a circuit as to continue his route southwards to Kársekhó, and then ascend a stream in order to reach a point to which he might have gone directly by land? And besides, the left bank of the Joliba, within the limits wherein we may reasonably look for the site of Málí, has been travelled over by Mungo Park, who found there no tributary stream. The mention of the river Ṣanṣarah, therefore, presents difficulties which admit of only one explanation. A great river like the Joliba, periodically overflowing the adjacent country, will probably form many channels, and insulate, perhaps by permanent canals, long tracts of low land, as is exemplified on a small scale in the course of the Medway below Chatham. Now, if we suppose that Málí stood in a low tract, intersected by a canal of the Joliba, called Ṣanṣarah,

---

132 Leo Africanus, pt. VII. c. 3 & 4.

then Ibn Baṭúṭah's movements may be easily explained. That the banks of the Joliba are almost impassable in the rainy season we know from the narrative of Park, who, being a stranger in the country, struggled through difficulties which a native perhaps would never have thought of encountering. But Ibn Baṭúṭah had an experienced guide; going to Málí, therefore, at the commencement of the rains (the end of June), he directed his course to an easily accessible point of the Joliba, and thence proceeded to the capital by the canal: leaving Málí in the middle of the dry season (the last day of February) he mounted his camel and crossed the country. Moreover, we are fortunately able to show that our hypothesis respecting the Ṣanṣarah, is not only not unnatural nor improbable, but that it truly represents the physical character of that part of the Joliba now under consideration, and that there is, in fact, a canal or arm of the river in the very place where we should expect to find the Ṣanṣarah. Mungo Park, describing his voyage down the Joliba from Samee to Sego, says, "We passed down a small stream to the north of Sego-korro, and halted opposite to Sego-sikorro, near the sandhills, where I formerly waited for a passage." In explanation of these words, it must be observed that Sego-korro is on the northern bank of the river; Sego-sikorro, where the King of Bambara resided, on the southern bank. The small stream north of Sego-korro, therefore, down which the traveller passed, (in the middle of August, when the floods were at their height,) must have been a canal or arm of the river insulating the ground on which Sego-korro stood.[33] Park

[33] Park's First Journey, p. 195. In the Rec. des Voy. tom. II. p. 53, it is maintained that all the villages composing Sego are on the right or southern bank of the river. But the general character of the information there given will not bear to be weighed against the clear testimony of Park. It seems not improbable that Kársekhó was a part of Sego, but there is no necessity for insisting on that point. Perhaps if Caillié, who applied the Wolof term *Marigot*, which he had learned in Senegal, to all the creeks of the Great River, had inquired how they were called in Bambara, or lower down, he might have learned the name Ṣanṣarah. Perhaps, too, the Gozen-zaire of Sidi Hamed's narrative (Riley, Loss of the Brig Commerce, p. 362), might have been more correctly written Go-sansarah. It seems to owe its present form to Riley's partiality to the hypothesis uniting the Niger with the Zaire.

does not state the length of the ***small stream***, nor say whether he entered it near Samee; but these particulars are here of little consequence, since our object is not to identify the small stream of Park with the Ṣanṣarah of Ibn Baṭúṭah, but only to show how perfectly our hypothesis respecting the latter harmonizes with nature and with fact. Yet it must not be concealed that there is reason for believing that the site of the capital of Málí was near Samee. Ibn Khaldún writes the proper name of that capital in characters wanting, unfortunately, the diacritic points; but these being supplied by probable conjecture, the passage in question will run thus: "And the residence of the king of the people of Málí is the city of ***Benní***," (or Benna).[134] A place called Binni, of little importance, stands on the north bank of the Joliba, about seven miles above Samee.

The sequel of Ibn Baṭúṭah's journey shall be related in his own words, though with some curtailment. He thus proceeds:—"We came to a wide creek or arm of the Nile, which can be crossed only in boats, on the third night after we left Málí. On arriving at its banks, I beheld, with astonishment, about sixteen immense animals, which I took to be elephants. However, when I saw them plunge into the water, I called out to Abú Bekr Ibn Yakúb, and asked him what are these? And he replied, 'They are river horses (Hippopotami), which come ashore to feed.' They are much larger than common horses, yet resemble them in their heads and the fulness of their manes, but their feet are like those of elephants. On another occasion, when navigating the river from Tomboktú to Kaúkaú, I had a view of these animals. They were swimming about with their heads above the water, and snorting. The natives attack them with javelins, to which are attached a number of cords. If the animal be struck in the neck or the leg, he is soon overcome, dragged to the bank, and killed. The natives eat the flesh, and the banks of the river are strewed over with the bones of these animals.[35]

---

[134] In the original thus: وحاضرَة الملك الاهل مالي هُوَ بلد بنى

[35] The wide arm of the river (Khalíj) reached by our traveller on the third night after his leaving Málí must have been the branch observed by Caillié to join the

"At this arm of the Nile we rested in a village governed by a negro named Farbá Maghá, one of those who had accompanied Mansá Músa on his pilgrimage. He related to us, that when Mansá Músa came to this place, he gave to Abú-l-Abbas Aldukálí, a white man and Kadhi who attended him, 4,000 mithkáls for the expenses of his journey. Abú-l-Abbas, however, on arriving at Mímah, complained that his money was stolen. The King thereupon sent for the governor, and threatened him with death, if the money and the thief were not immediately discovered. The search seemed at first fruitless; but on the slaves of Abú-l-Abbas being menaced and strictly questioned, one of them, a young girl, pointed out the spot where her master had buried the money. Mansá Músa, on hearing this, banished the Kadhi to the country of the Unbelievers, who eat men. There he stayed four years, before he was permitted to return; and the Blacks did not eat him, because they say that white man's flesh is bad meat, being flabby and immature. And here I must relate a curious anecdote. Some of these cannibals, led by a chief, came on a certain occasion to the court of Mansá Suleïmán; they were clothed in silk wrappers, and had enormous pendants in their ears, the holes in which were an inch in diameter. The King received them with much distinction, regaled them sumptuously, and, as a token of regard, gave them a slave girl. They immediately killed the girl, and ate her; then, besmearing their hands and faces with her blood, they visited the Sultan, and thanked him for his present. In the country of these cannibals there are mines of gold.[36]

"Leaving the village on the water side, we came to Korí Mansá, where the camel that I was riding died. When my

---

river from the west at Isaca. He supposed it to come from Sego (Voy. à Temboctou, p. 239), but its separation from the main stream must be lower down. There is, as yet, no sufficient reason to deny that the river of Sego is also the river of Jenni, and that the latter place stands between its branches, and not between two distinct rivers.

[36] This anecdote, like most stories of cannibalism, has the defect of not proceeding from an eye witness; but it proves one fact, namely, that the people of Málí were not cannibals.

servant told me of this accident, I went out to witness it with my own eyes, and there I beheld the Blacks already devouring the carcass, their custom being to eat every kind of dead animal. I then sent two of my followers to a town called Zagharí, about two days' journey from Korí Mansá, to buy me another camel. In six days they returned, and we then took the road to Mímah. We did not enter that town, however, but encamped outside near the wells. Thence we arrived at Tomboktú, a city four miles distant from the Nile. Most of its inhabitants are people of Mímah, or of the tribes called Almolaththemún. One day I went to visit the governor, Farbá Músa, and met at his house a Masúfí, who had just arrived in Tomboktú, to take the command of the people of his tribe established there. The governor gave him a robe, a turban, and pair of trowsers, all of figured cotton; and made him sit on a shield, while the chief people of his tribe lifted him above their heads.[137]

"At Tomboktú I embarked in a small canoe made of a single trunk of a tree, and went down the river. We landed every night, and went to some inhabited place to procure what we wanted,—such as oil, and other necessaries—giving in exchange for them salt, drugs, and trinkets. We came to a place, the name of which I have forgotten, but where Farbá Suleïmán, a Hájí of sterling worth, was governor. He was a man of great size and strength, and had a bow which none of the Blacks but himself could bend. I went into his house to ask for a little durrah, and my request being interpreted for him by a faḳíh who was present, he took me by the hand, and led me into his principal chamber, which was filled with arms of various kinds, shields, bows, and javelins. There was then brought to me a drink called Aldaḳnó, prepared from bruised

---

[137] Korí Mansá كُرِي منسا. Perhaps this place was the residence of the chief (Mansá) who levied the tax on cotton (Korí). The name written in the original Rárí رعري has been here changed into Zagharí (See above, p. 75), as the existence of two places not far asunder, and with names written so much alike, is much less probable than a lapse in the MSS. Mímah ميمه is the Amímah of older writers.

durrah, with milk and honey. We then ate of a water melon; and in conclusion, a young slave coming into the room, Farbá Suleïmán presented him to me, and I have him at the present day.[38]

"From this place we went on to Kaúkaú, one of the largest, handsomest, and strongest cities in all Negroland. It stands on the banks of the Nile, and abounds in rice, milk, poultry, fish, and fruit of matchless excellence. The people there, as well as in Málí,use shells for money. I stayed in Kaúkaú about two months, and then went by land in the direction of Tekaddá, with a large Káfilah of people of Ghodémis.[39] We came into the country of the Berdámah, a Berber tribe, whose protection and friendship are indispensable for the safety of travellers in this region. The Berdámah are wanderers, and never remain long in one place. Their tents are of a peculiar construction; they fix poles in the ground, and place on them a matting of reeds; over this they form a trellis-work of boughs of trees, and cover the frame thus constructed with skins and cotton cloths. Their women are the prettiest and best shaped that I have ever seen; they are as white as snow, and the fattest in the world. Whoever wishes to have a woman of this tribe, needs only to go to the wells near their encampments in the evening, and she will be sure to follow him; but he must not take her further than Kaúkaú or Aïwalátin.[40]

"We continued our march to Tekaddá, where the houses are built of red stone; the water is coloured by running over copper ores, which impart to it a disagreeable flavour. The people of Tekaddá sow no grain; they are wholly devoted to trade, and live in affluence; their luxury consisting, as in Málí and Aïwalátin, in slaves of both sexes, of whom some classes

---

38 The Daḳnó of Ibn Baṭúṭah is the Dokhnou of Caillié:—"Un mélange de farine de mil et de miel que l'on délaie pour ensuite le boire." (Voy. à Temb. II. p. 236.) This word belongs apparently to the Kissour language.

39 The word here rendered merchants of Godémis, is Ḳodémiyín قدامسين.

40 The Berdámah بردامة were probably a family of the Beghámah, a nomade tribe mentioned by El Idrísí, whose country lay behind that of the Merásah, to the east of Ghánah.

fetch exorbitant prices. The king of Tekaddá is a Berber. The copper taken from the mines near the town is made into small bars about an inch and a half thick, which are exchanged for grain, meat, fuel, and other necessaries. These bars are carried to Kúber, in the country of the Infidels, to Rághá, and to Bornú, which is forty days' journey from Tekaddá. The king of that country (who is named Idris) never speaks to his subjects, unless from behind a screen or curtain.[141]

"From Tekaddá we set forward on our march to Twát, which is seventy days distant, and came to Káhir, which belongs to the Sultan of Karkar, and yields sufficient pasturage. Then going three days over a waterless desert, and fifteen through a tract uninhabited but not waterless, we came to the place where the road to Egypt separates from that to Twat. The water of the wells in that place being impregnated with iron, stains linen. In ten days more we came to Dekhár, and in another month reached Búdá, one of the largest towns of Twát."

To the foregoing narrative a few remarks may be here advantageously subjoined. If it be granted that Ibn Baṭúṭah, in sending to Zagharí for a camel to replace that which died at Korí Mansá, had recourse to the nearest town, then it follows that Mímah, one stage at least from Tomboktú, must have been more than two stages from Korí Mansá. But this place, in a mean position, will be nearly as far as Zagharí, or fourteen days, from the capital of Mální. This capital must therefore have been, at the lowest calculation, eighteen days from Tomboktú.[42]

It is worthy of attention, that, in the fourteenth century, Tomboktú was peopled chiefly by natives of Mímah, and by the Molaththemún, the very parties with whom Ghánah, three

---

[141] Ibn Baṭúṭah himself bought a female slave at Tekaddá for twenty-five mithḳáls, no exorbitant price apparently. Kúber كوبر. Rághá راغا. Káhir كاهر. Of Karkar some notice will be taken hereafter.

[42] Cadamosto learned that Málí was thirty days from Tomboktú. The last-named city is generally said to be ten days from Jenni by land, and twenty-five by water; but the land journeys here meant cannot be those of a loaded caravan, but nearly half as long again. Sego is five or six days above Jenni.

centuries before, had to maintain a constant warfare. The Masúfah, the early occupants of the desert between Sijilmésah and Ghánah, extended from Tegháza to Tomboktú, and mercenary bands of them were at the court of Málí. But the caravan road seems to have been their only territory; eastward they were bounded by the Berdámah, who carried water for sale into the desert of Azawad, and whose encampments were probably not ten days distant from Tomboktú.

There does not appear to have been any place of note between Tomboktú and Kaúkaú; nor does Ibn Baṭúṭah say a word favourable to the supposition that the former of these cities was in his time intrinsically important. Kaúkaú, on the other hand, then enjoyed that eminence among the cities of Negroland which it continued to retain for at least four centuries.[43] The morals of the Berdámah, of Aïwalátin, and Tekaddá, as described by Ibn Baṭúṭah, bear a close resemblanee to those characterizing Aúdaghost and Tádmekkah in earlier times, and indicate the same fundamental conditions of society. The women of the Berdámah, he says, were willing to follow strangers, on the implied condition that they were not to be taken beyond Kaúkaú or Aïwalátin. This is as much as to say, that they willingly accompanied merchants arriving with the Káfilahs from the north-east, to a certain distance on either of the two frequented roads; but it is remarkable that no mention is here made of a road to any part of Houssa.

Tekaddá was seventy days from Twát, and as fifty-eight of these are accounted for, we may conclude that Tekaddá was twelve days from Káhir, and thirty from the place where the roads to Twát and Egypt divided (probably near Ghát); it was also forty days from Bornú, so that its position may be ascertained with sufficient accuracy. Leo Africanus states, that beyond or eastward of the Desert of the Zenágah lay that of the Zuenziga, "which extends from the neighbourhood of

[43] It is fortunate that Ibn Khaldún removes all doubts as to the identity of Ibn Baṭúṭah's Kaúkaú with Leo's Gago. The latter writer calls it (pt. VII. c. 7) "una grandissima citta." He also says that, compared with the rest of Negroland, it was "molto civile." His list of prices is curious, as well as his Macchiavellian remark on the ignorance and oppressed condition of the lower orders.

Tegaza eastwards, to the borders of the Desert of Air, inhabited by the Targa (Tawárik); and from the confines of Segelmessa, Tebelbelt, and Benigomi southwards (south-eastwards), to the Desert of Ghir, which is opposite to the kingdom of Guber." It has been already shown that by Air Leo meant the Desert of 'Ahír east of Aghades; and it seems equally certain that his Ghir is the Káhir of Ibn Baṭúṭah.[144] The copper of Tekaddá was taken to Bornú, Kúber (Guber), and Rághá (Raka in Yariba?); and here it is worthy of remark, that Guber, the frontier province of Houssa towards the desert, and the province to which native historians concede the superiority derivable from an early intercourse with white men, was still pagan in the fourteenth century. This fact alone would be sufficient to prove that Houssa formed no part of the Negroland which fell within the range of the Morabites, even if the general tenor of their history did not contradict such an extension of their conquests; or if the question were not decided by the authority of Ibn Khaldún, who says expressly that "Tekaddá was behind the country of the Morabites."[45]

Ibn Baṭúṭah makes no allusion to the extent of the empire of Málí towards the west or south; but he clearly indicates its limits towards the north and east. When first mentioning the river, he describes its course in the following terms:—"We came to the Great River, which is the Nile, and on the banks of which stands the city of Kársekhó. Thence the Nile descends to Kábrah and to Zághah, and the Sultans of these

---

[144] When Ibn Khaldún says that Tekaddá is seventy days south-west of Wergelán (see p. 65), it is evident that he measures the circuitous route by Ghát; and that the bearing of Tekaddá from Ghát is incautiously taken by him for the direction of the whole journey.

[45] The superiority of the people of Guber is plainly asserted by Sultan Bello, who says (Appendix to Denham and Clapperton's Travels, 8vo. II. p. 450) that they alone, of all the Houssa tribes, are free born, being descended from the Copts, while the rest are the progeny of Bawwa, or Baúwa, that is, a slave (not Ba-oo, as in Mr. Salamé's Translation). The country of the Baúwa is Baúchi, or Baúji, commonly written Bowshee. Sultan Bello's History, brought to Europe by Clapperton, would well deserve a critical study: but where is the original? Did it belong to the public? and if it did, why is it not in the library of the British Museum?

two cities are tributary to the Sultan of Málí. The inhabitants of Zághah were the first [in these countries] who embraced Mohammedism. They are religious, and fond of learning. From Zághah the river descends to Tomboktú; thence to Kaúkaú; thence to the district of Múlí, in the country of the Límiyín, which terminates [in that direction] the dominion of Málí. It goes thence to Yúfí (Núfí), one of the greatest states in Negroland, and the Sultan of which is among the most powerful princes of that quarter of the earth. No white man can reach that country, for sure death awaits him from the natives before he penetrates so far. From Yúfí the Nile descends to Nubia, the inhabitants of which are Christians, and to Dongolah," &c.[46]

---

[46] The Arabic MS. here varies a little in its readings. It says—"from Kársekhó the Nile descends to Kabúrah كَبُورة and to Zághah زاغة; and these two cities, namely, al-Kábrah الكابرة and Zághíah زاغية, pay tribute to Málí." Tomboktú تنبكتوا is carefully spelt by Ibn Baṭúṭah, the letters with which it is written being named by him, with their vowel points. Ibn Baṭúṭah never alludes to the native names of the Great River, but always calls it the Nile. The local names of the theoretical Niger (the Senegal and Great River together) collected by De Barros (Dec. I. liv. 3, c. 8), do not contain the Mandingo name Joliba. This name was first announced to the geographical world when speculation was unusually active, and it was immediately explained to mean *the Great Waters.* Park, though he seems to have adopted this interpretation (Travels, p. 194), can hardly be supposed to have been its author. Laing joins the statement of his precursors to his own information, and says (Travels, p. 327), that the Niger "is known by the synonymous appellations of Ba Ba and Joli Ba—"*Large River.*" Ba Bá certainly signifies Great River, the substantive *Ba*, a river, preceding the adjective *Bá*, great, according to the general rule of the Mandingo language. Thus in Ba-fing, black river, Ba-koé, white river, Ba-woollima, red river, the word *Ba*, a river, has precedence; but when joined with a substantive, as in Kuara-ba, the river of Kuara, it follows. With these examples before our eyes, it is impossible to admit the explanation of the name of Joliba given above, which receives moreover no support from the vocabularies. It is likely that the name Joliba, or, as written by Caillié, Dhioliba, by Mollien, Dialiba, means the river of the Jál or Jolá, Juli, Jaules, Diaules, or Dhioli (red men), from whose country it descends, whether its sources be, as stated by Park (Travels, App. p. xliv.), in Jallonké-dú, *i. e.* Jallo-man's land, or in Bé-dú, where are the Juli towns and men of a red complexion.

Notwithstanding the confusion into which the writer of Ibn Baṭúṭah's narrative here falls, placing Zághah below Kábrah, evidently in ignorance of the proximity of the latter place to Tomboktú, yet as we know that Zághah was not on the part of the river which Ibn Baṭúṭah actually navigated, viz. between Tomboktú and Kaúkaú, we may rest satisfied that it was above Kábrah. The empire of Málí extended along both banks of the Great River as far as Tomboktú. On the left it stretched northward to the border of the desert and the route of the caravans, thus comprising the territory of the ancient Ghánah. Eastward of Tomboktú it appears to have been bounded by the river; the Berdámah and other tribes of the desert on the left bank retaining their independence. Kaúkaú had been annexed to the empire, but no advance made eastwards from that place, nor had Tekaddá been as yet invaded. Below Kaúkaú the river flowed by the district of Múlí in the country of the Límiyín (who were on its left bank, as shall be shown hereafter), and at that point terminated, towards the east, the empire of Málí.

The Múlí of Ibn Baṭúṭah is apparently the district called by Mohammed Masíní Mouri (Múrí), four long days' journey west of Sokkatú. It is said to be mountainous and well watered; it immediately adjoins the Desert of the Tawárik, and its inhabitants are still pagans. It is therefore the northern limit of the negro population on the left bank of the Kowára, or on the side of Houssa.[147]

---

147 Beldeh Múlí بلدة مولي. The Fellátah geographer wrote sometimes Mouri (Appendix to Clapperton's Second Journey, p. 332), sometimes (p. 340) Mouli (Múlí). He says, that the people of Núfí conquered, among other countries, "the west of Malee, or Moulee, and Abyou." And again, that they subdued "the country of Abbi (in which we now are) and Kanbari" (Kombori). Abbi is probably the same as Abyou (or rather Abbíwa), and appears to have been near Sokkatú. In Hannah Kilham's Specimens of Languages spoken in Sierra Leone, we find the Appah and Tapua, both related to the Aku or Yariba. The Tapua is evidently the Tappawa, or language of Núfí (called Tappa by its inhabitants), and the Appah is perhaps the language of Abbi. One of the native itineraries appended to Dupuis' Residence in Ashantee (p. cxxix.), places Maury (Múri) next to Kábi on the west.

By the possession of Múlí the people of Málí had ready ingress into the countries whence slaves were taken, but there is no authority whatever for the supposition that they ever extended their dominion further eastward; and care must be taken, therefore, not to confound the Mandingo empire of Málí with the country called Marra or Malla, situate on the confines of the former in the north-western part of Houssa. It seems clearly ascertained that the north-west part of Houssa, or the territory between Zanfara and the Kowára, is called by the natives Marra, or by those who affect the Arab sounds, Malla. The ancient greatness assigned to Marra in the historical traditions of the natives, favours the opinion that it was the Melil or Malilo of the early Arab writers. At present the name Marra is used only by the indigenous population, and it is curious to observe that its former importance never brought it to the ears of Clapperton or Lander. But its partial obscurity only renders it more likely to lead to confusion; and therefore, in order to distinguish clearly between Málí and Malla, let it be observed, that the former of these lay on the west of the Kowára, the latter on the east. Málí was the empire of the Mandingoes; Malla a kingdom of Houssa. These two states approached, and may have met each other near Múlí; but there is no positive ground for believing that they were in any degree connected, or that the conquests of Málí ever extended into Malla.[48]

Opposite to Múlí, or on the right bank of the Kowára, the dominion of Málí probably extended a little southward to the

---

[48] From Marra is formed the gentile noun Marrawa; just as Asbenawa is derived from Asben, Kachenawa from Kachena, Killiwawa from Killiwah. But the carelessness of authors has given to the country the name Marrawa, Mallawa, or Marroa, which properly belongs to the people. According to Dupuis (Resid. in Ashantee, App. lxxxviii.), Marroa was conquered by the Arabs at the close of the eighth century of our era. For Melil see p. 37. Bowdich (Essay on the Geogr. of N.W. Afr. p. 24) has laboured to show that Mallawa (or Malla) is the Melli of Leo, or Málí; and Dalzel (History of Dahomy, p. 34) speaks of a people of the interior called Malays or Mulays; but though the resemblance of the names Malla, Melli or Málí, and Múlí, favours confusion, all that we know of their application is on the side of discrimination.

borders of Bergú. Ibn Baṭúṭah relates that Bálbá Ḳásá, the queen of Mansá Suleïmán, sent, in a fit of displeasure, a confidential messenger to Mári Jáṭah, the King's nephew, instigating him to revolt, and promising to gain over the army to his interest. Mári Jáṭah was at that time governor of Kombori.[149] Now this name occurs in the fragments of native geographers collected by Capt. Clapperton. It is therein stated that Kanbari (Kombori) lies north of the River Kadúna; and again, we are told, that the river of that country is called Kantagoora (Kotú-n-kúra). Yet the Kombori, of which Jáṭah was governor, could not have been the country on the river of Kotú-n-kúra, for this is beyond Múlí, where the dominion of Málí terminated. This objection may be removed, however, by a little attention to the comprehensiveness of the name under consideration. Clapperton informs us that the aboriginal inhabitants of the country of Boussa (Busá) are the negroes called Cambrie or Cumbrie (Kombori), who still preserve their own language, and dwell in the woods on both sides of the river, their villages extending also a long way up the Kotú-n-kúra. From them, therefore, it is evident that the country on this river takes the name of Kombori. But they also occupy all the islands in the river above Busá, and are the

---

149 Ibn Baṭúṭah relates the transaction above alluded to with many details illustrative of the manners of Málí. The King, it appears, grew tired of his chief wife, Bálbá Ḳásá, who, by the custom of the country, shared his authority: (Ḳásá, the Caza of old vocabularies, means Queen;) he therefore placed her in confinement in the house of one of his Farárí or captains, and took for queen in her stead his other wife Banjú, who was not of the blood royal. The people manifested dissatisfaction at this change. The female relatives of the King, in visiting Banjú, put dust on their elbows, but not on their heads. When Bálbá Ḳásá, however, was soon after released from confinement, the same parties presented themselves before her with their heads covered with dust and ashes. Thereupon Banjú complained that the deposed queen was treated with more honour than herself. Mansá Suleïmán was incensed; and his relatives, fearing his vengeance, fled to the sanctuary. He soon pardoned them, however, and then the ladies, according to custom, presented themselves before him naked. But the public discontent with the King continued to increase, till one day the Royal Interpreter Dúghá led forth before the assembly a young female slave in chains, who disclosed the conspiracy above related. It was then agreed that Bálbá Ḳásá deserved death.

indigenous inhabitants of the territory of Busá, which extends eleven days' journey northwards up the right bank of the Kowára. They occupy, therefore, the country opposite to Múlí, where we may accordingly place with much probability the province of Kombori belonging to Málí.[50]

"From Múlí (says Ibn Baṭúṭah) the river descends to Yúfí (Núfí), one of the greatest kingdoms of Negroland, but to which white men cannot penetrate; and thence it flows to Nubia." It would appear, from this, that the superiority now enjoyed by the people of Núfí in arts and industry, was already acknowledged in the fourteenth century. It is manifest also that the system of the native geographers which converts the Chadda into a continuation of the Kowára, by which the waters of this great river are carried across Bornú to the Nile of Egypt, is of some antiquity. Ibn Baṭúṭah believed that the great river below Múlí flowed some distance to the south or south-east before it turned eastwards to Nubia. In speaking of Kulwá (Kilwá, or Quiloa), on the eastern coast of Africa, he uses these words:—"A merchant there told me, that the town of Sofálah is half a month's journey from Kulwá, and one month from Yúfí in the country of the Límiyín, and that gold is brought from Yúfí to Sofálah."[51] The boldness here evinced in bringing together and joining in commerce countries far asunder, is constantly exhibited in the geographical speculations of an early or ill-informed age. Distances are then enlarged as expediency requires; hypothesis leaps over the vacant spaces, and forcibly stretches the known portions in the opposite sides of a continent till they meet in the centre. Illustrations of this truth may be found in all ages. During the sixteenth and seventeenth centuries, Abyssinia, Congo, and

---

[50] The situation of Kanbari (Kombori) is described in the Appendix to Clapperton's Second Expedition, pp. 339 & 340. For some account of the people who give their name to this country, see Clapperton's Narrative, pp. 97, 102, 147, &c.; and also Lander's Expedition to the Niger, II. pp. 87, 299.

[51] For Yúfí يوفي Professor Lee (Travels of Ibn Baṭúṭah, p. 238) reads Yúwí, and Burckhardt (Travels in Nubia, p. 491) Bowy. It is obviously Núfí mis-pointed.

Monomotapa were all supposed to meet together. One of the Jesuits resident in Abyssinia asserts, that salt was carried from that country to Tomboktú.[152] The reasoning which led to this statement was, in its nature, exactly the same as that from which the Arabs inferred an intercourse between Sofálah and Yúfí. It is not surprising, therefore, that Ibn Baṭúṭah, who had far less accurate means of ascertaining the true positions of the places visited by him than the Catholic missionaries, should believe that the remote interior, whence gold was brought to Sofálah, was occupied by the same nation who filled the interior viewed in the opposite direction from Málí. Erroneous as this kind of inference may be, it yet rests on ideas of direction so manifest and unambiguous as to be of material service in explaining an author's meaning. It is plain, then, that Ibn Baṭúṭah thought Yúfí to lie between Málí and Sofálah, and that the Great River from Múlí to Yúfí flowed towards Sofálah, but beyond Yúfí turned eastwards to Nubia.

It is impossible to quit the narrative of Ibn Baṭúṭah's travels without making an important reflection on the extent and direction of his journey to Negroland. We see in him an enterprising, experienced, well-informed traveller, whose ambition it was, apparently, to explore all the known parts of the earth; he goes from Sijilmésah across the desert to Málí, thence to Tomboktú, and then descends the river as far as Kaúkaú, and from Kaúkaú he turns off north-eastwards to the Desert on his way back. Now can it be reasonably doubted that, in this tour, he visited *the Negroland* with which Sijilmésah had maintained an intercourse from the earliest times, and which had been so minutely described by El Bekrí and

---

152 In like manner the supposed Christian King named Ogané, of whom the early Portuguese navigators received intelligence at Benin, was at once assumed to be the King of Abyssinia. The fable of an intercourse between Abyssinia and Western Africa has been gravely repeated by a recent writer (M'Queen's Survey of Africa, p. 5). Fernandez de Enciso (Suma de Geografia, 1518) says, that in the Bight of Benin are the Blacks who trade with Libya and Meroe. Lalande (Mémoires de Paris, 1795, p. 15) has collected with equal industry and credulity the stories of an overland commerce between the eastern and western coasts of Africa.

others? Can it be doubted that he accomplished his proposed task in the sense in which it was understood by his countrymen, and that the Negroland of western writers consequently lay between the capital of Málí and Kaúkaú or Kághó? When he alludes to Gúber as a pagan country, but says nothing of Kanó, can it be seriously maintained that he slightingly passes over in silence the only part of Negroland described with copious and connected details by the best Arab writers?

The hypothesis identifying Kanó with Ghánah appears to have originated with Leo Africanus, and rests on no better foundation than the supposed resemblance of those names, which to an impartial critic must appear widely dissimilar.[53] Neither can it be admitted that Aghades was ever called

---

[53] Leo says (pt. VII. c. 1), "Our ancient writers on Africa, as El Bekrí and El Mesúdí, have written nothing respecting any part of Negroland, except el Waḥat (the Oases) and Cano." This sentence, which has been of course copied with little change by Marmol (tom. III. fol. 21), can be explained only by supposing that Cano (Kanó) here means Ghánah. However ill-considered or obscurely intimated may be Leo's opinion, it yet probably influenced not a little the decision of D'Anville in favour of the identity of Kanó with Ghánah. Major Rennell most unaccountably assumes that by Cano Leo meant the town of Ganat (or rather Janat), between Fezzan and Ghát. Perhaps the latter writer's statement that "Cano is a great province, about 500 miles distant from the Niger towards the east," contained something incompatible with the Major's system, and made it absolutely necessary for him to expel Leo's Cano from Negroland. Major Rennell disserted always shrewdly, and sometimes with a very imperfect knowledge of his authors. Thus he asserts that, under the name Genni (Jenni), Leo meant to describe Ghánah; and that he was wrong in placing Genni or Ghánah, and Melli, west of Tomboktú, "for Leo certainly never saw the Niger." Now Leo, when he speaks of Genni, says that it is the name used by the natives, and derives it (with little reason) from Gheneoa (Genéwa), a name as ancient as Ghánah, and quite distinct from it. Moreover Leo not only saw the Niger, but actually navigated it to Jenni and Málí (pt. I. c. 3). It is not easy to discover from Major Rennell's dissertations the position assigned by him to Ghánah, but his map shows that he confounded it with Kanó. These two names, as pronounced in Africa, have much less resemblance in sound than is commonly imagined. Written in Arabic, they have but one letter in common. Ghánah begins with a peculiar sonorous guttural, which is followed by a long vowel; Kanó is like our word canoe. Einsiedel (Cuhn's Merkwürdige Reisen, vol. III. p. 435) writes it *Gnou*.

Aúdaghost, or that it is only twenty-five days from Jermah in Fezzán. Kanó is two months from Jermah, four or five months from the Western Ocean, and an equal distance from Sijilmésah, with which country it certainly never maintained any intercourse. It is not close to the desert, nor is there any desert of extreme aridity within much less than a month's journey from it.[154] It has no navigable river near it, nor even any stream which is not quite dry in summer; much less can the series of names placed on the river of Ghánah be found in its vicinity. Neither do the descriptions of Ghánah, with all their details, contain the names of any of the countries near Kanó. The tribes of the desert on the frontiers of Houssa have all come from the neighbourhood of Fezzán, and not from Sijilmésah.[55] Kanó is removed far from the deserts of the Zenágah and of the Morabites, who always hung over Ghánah, and at length became its masters: nor was Kanó included in the empire of Málí when this power had attained its greatest extension, and had advanced far beyond Ghánah. To one who examines with patience and attention the accounts of Ghánah, it cannot but appear surprising that its identity with Kanó should be maintained and acquiesced in even at the present day.

---

[154] In order to prove that Kanó was the Ghánah of early writers, it was necessary to assume not only the close resemblance of those names, but also that the name Aghades was a corruption of Aúdaghost. Then the distance between this place and Jermah, according to El Idrísí, is called in as a confirmation. A single particular is taken from that writer, all the others with which it stands connected being disregarded, though the rejected details are founded on experience, and the retained one on inference alone. Yet this arbitrary reasoning cannot after all attain its desired ends. Aghades is not twenty-five but forty-five days from Jermah, and Kanó is not twelve but twenty-eight days from Aghades (Walckenaer Rech. p. 448; Lyon's Trav. p. 131). The deserts of 'Ahír and Káhir, beyond Aghades, are far from being utterly inhospitable tracts.

[55] According to Sultan Bello (Denham and Clapperton's Disc. 8vo. II. p. 447), the people of Guber at one time held possession of the Desert of 'Ahír, but were dispossessed by five tribes of the Tawárik, who came out of Aowjal (Augila).

TEKRÚR.

Ibn Baṭúṭah, in describing the course of the Great River below Kársekhó, makes no mention of Tekrúr, the first converted of the Negro communities in that quarter. That designation, though widely and vaguely extended in process of time, was certainly at first applied to a spot between Silla and Ṣínghánah, and not far from the former of these places. Wárjání, the chief of Tekrúr who first adopted the Mohammedan faith, and induced his subjects to follow his example, died in 432 H. (A.D. 1040-1); so that the conversion of his principality preceded, by thirty-five years at least, that of Ghánah and Western Negroland in general. Such a priority explains at once the religious eminence implied in the title Tekrúr (whatever may have been its original signification), and which caused it to be usurped till its proper application was at length forgotten.[56]

But though Ibn Baṭúṭah does not expressly mention Tekrúr, yet he says of Zághah, situate between Kársekhó and Tomboktú, that it was the first city of Negroland which received the Mohammedan faith. Hence it may be inferred that Zághah was the proper territorial name of the place styled Tekrúr. And this conjecture receives from Ibn Khaldún strong confirmation, falling short of completeness only through the unsteady orthography which so often hinders the exact coincidence of Arab authorities. His words are as follows: —"I was told by the Sheíkh 'Othmán, a learned man and theologian of the people of Ghánah, and one of the chief men of that country in respect to rank, intelligence, and piety, when he came to Egypt on his way to Mekkah in 796 (A.D. 1393),

[56] Tekrúr, according to El Bekrí (Not. et Extr. tom. XII. p. 637), was at no great distance from Ṣínghánah towards the south-west. El Idrísí always unites Silla and Tekrúr. The date of Wárjání's death is given by El Bekrí (MS. B.M. fol. 110), who also states that the people of Silla embraced Mohammedism at that chief's persuasion. Wárjání was probably a Zenágah, a great number of proper names in the Berber language beginning with the syllable *wer* or *wár* (the negative particle?). A prince of Tekrúr accompanied the Lumtúnah in their first religious wars.

that the people of Ghánah employ the name Tekrúr to designate the Zagháï, and give the name Málí to Atakárthah." —It can hardly be doubted that the people here called Zagháï derived their name from the place called by Ibn Baṭúṭah Zághah. The name Atakárthah does not admit of quite so easy an explanation; yet it may with much probability be assumed to be the original and complete Berber form of the name, now written in our maps, Kaarta. The statement of the Sheíkh 'Othmán then amounts to this: the people of Ghánah discriminated, in terms naturally arising out of their local position, between Tekrúr and Málí, giving the former name to a certain tribe dwelling to the south, and the latter to a particular region higher up the river, and the frontier of which, facing Ghánah, was Atakárthah or Kaarta.[157]

The country of Tekrúr or of the Zagháï thus discriminated from Málí, which lay further west, may be clearly recognized in modern accounts, notwithstanding the disguise of a variable orthography. Sultan Bello, after describing the country of

---

157 The name Zaghái زغاي cannot, it is true, be formed from Zághah زاغة; but considering that they are taken from different authors, and that the orthography of African names is extremely unsettled, there is no great boldness in the hypothesis which connects them. It is easier to believe that one of these names requires a little correction, than that the Tekrúrí did not bear the name of the town which first received the Mohammedan faith. Makrízí, or Ibn Sáíd, from whom he copies, says (Hamaker, Specimen Catalogi, &c., p. 209,) "that all the nations comprised between Abyssinia on the south, Nubia on the east, Barkah on the north, and Tekrúr on the west, are called Zagháï." Here the name Zagháï is derived from Zagháwah, and the Tekrúr spoken of is that of Houssa. An anecdote related in the 'History of the Mohammedan Dynasties,' by Gayangos (p. 303), shows that in the thirteenth century, there was a state called Tekrúr in the neighbourhood of Aïwalátin. An Arab writer of little merit apparently (in the Library of the British Museum, MS. No. 7,483), says that "the Blacks are now in general styled Tekrúr; but anciently the name Tekrúr was applied only to the inhabitants of the country called Atasama اتّسمى." It may be conjectured that Atasama is an ill-written derivative from S̈ámah, the country of the Bokmo or Bagamo. The *t* is a Berber article; the initial *a* the sign of the possessive case, and perhaps also of adjectives derived therefrom. Thus the Berbers say, Mohammed a-Mohammed a-Mast, to express Mohammed, son of Mohammed, of or belonging to Messah. Hence also from Mazig, the reputed ancestor of the Berbers, and personification of the μαζίκες of the Greeks, was formed the name Amazig (see De Sacy's Analysis of

Mósí, thus proceeds:—"Adjoining to it on the north side, the province of Sanghee (Zághí) lies. Its inhabitants are remnants of the Sonhaja (Zenágah), wandering Arabs and the Felateen. They profess the Mohammedan faith, and their princes ruled them always with equity and justice. A great number of learned and pious persons have distinguished themselves from among them. Next to Sanghee on the west side, the country of Málí is situated. It embraces the province of Bambara," &c.[58]—The situation here assigned to Sanghee, and the reputed piety of its inhabitants, clearly show that it is the country of Tekrúr or of the Zagháï mentioned by Ibn Khaldún, and the Zághah or Zághiyah of Ibn Baṭúṭah. The commercial activity of the people, or perhaps their social ascendency due to their religious reputation, appears in the wide diffusion of their language; for, according to Leo, the *Sungai* (Zagháï) language was used in Walet, Tomboktú, Jenni, Málí, and Kághó.[59]

Shehabeddin in Not. et Extr. tom. II. p. 153, and the extract from Ibn Khaldún's History of the Berbers in the Nouv. Jour. Asiatique, No. VIII., 1828, p. 132). The reader may consider how far these remarks are applicable to such names as Atakárthah, Atasama, Amímah, and perhaps Awalílí or Aúlílí (see Note 103).

[58] For Mósí, the translator of Bello's History has written Moosher (Denham's Discoveries, &c. 8vo. II. p. 455), just as he has written Bowsher for Baúshí (p. 450). The Arabic letter *ghain*, here represented by *gh*, easily becomes nasal; and on the east coast of Africa, where the nasal sound occurs frequently in the native names, as in Songa, Tongata, Mongallo, it is always expressed by *ghain* alone. Hence Zághah in the mouth of a Mandingo, becomes Zanghah and Ṣanghah.

[59] Leo, pt. I. c. 11. Marmol (tom. I. c. 23, fol. 44) includes Gelofe (the country of the Wolofs), also within the range of the Zungay or Sungai language; but the origin of this mistake is perhaps not undiscoverable. He says (tom. III. fol. 22) that the people of Gualata or Ganata are commonly called Benais, and that they speak the Zungay language. Whence did the people of Gualata (Walata) obtain that name? Were they colonists from the capital of Málí? In the 'True Historical Discovery of Muley Hamet's Rising,' it is said that "the grasshoppers (locusts) come into Barbary every seven years from the parts of Benie, or Genie, as the country people imagine." Although the names Beni (Benin) and Guinea were often coupled together by old writers, yet it seems more natural to suppose that, in the passage here cited, the parts of Negroland nearest to Barbary were intended, and that by Benie, or Genie, we are to understand the country of Marmol's Benais, or Jenni. But Marmol (tom. I. fol. 2 & 15) also places a people named Benais on

The geographical sketch of Negroland drawn by Sultan Bello, differs materially from that made by his follower Mohammed Másíní, inasmuch as the former exhibits the territorial divisions of the indigenous population, whereas the latter offers only Fellátah names, and totally overlooks the aboriginal inhabitants. Nevertheless, the Zagháï, or people of Sanghee, are to be found in Mohammed's descriptions with little change of denomination. In describing the road from Sokkatú to Másín, he places, seven days east of the latter country, "the territory of Hajrí,"—that is, the rocky or mountainous tract. The Fellátah, he says, possess the valleys, "but the mountains are inhabited by a people called Benoo-Hami, of the tribe of Sokai (Zagháï), who are great warriors. In the middle of this country is a great and lofty mountain, on which is a town called Oonbori, whose king is named Noohoo-Ghaloo-farma, of the tribe of Sokai, and is renowned for his generosity and munificence." Further on we are told that Oonbori is comprised in the dominion of the Sultan of Másín, so that the people here called the tribe of Sokai probably extend from the mountains to the river. Alexander Scott received from his ignorant companions a distorted account of the Zachah (Zagháï) dwelling on the eastern shores of Lake Debú; and the town of Sankhaguibila, placed by Caillié on the right bank of the river farther south, appears to owe its name to the same tribe (Ḳabílah).[160]

---

the coast near the Senegal. In this, perhaps, he was guided by the Jesuit missionaries, who visited, from Cape Verde, a king of Bena (Ragguagli d'alcuni Missioni, 1615, p. 75); probably the Benay of Mollien. But the king of Bena was a Mandingo or Suso, and boasted of being superior to all other Farims (Jarric, tom. III. p. 411). Marmol appears to have confounded the Bena near the coast, with the Benai people of the interior, and thus to have made one language extend from the mouth of the Senegal to Houssa. Hence Moore, in his Travels in Africa, (1737), calls the Wolofe language the Zanguay.

[160] Oonbori, possessed by the Benú Hami of the tribe of Sokai (App. to Clapperton's Journal of a Second Expedition, p. 331), is probably the Anbárah of El Bekrí (see above, p. 39). It is to be observed, that the chief of Oonbori has the Mandingo title *Farma*, a remnant of the supremacy of Málí, following his name, contrary to the usage of the Mandingo language. If the *Sungai* then be the language of the Sokai, it is probably the same which Caillié calls the *Kissour*.

The Benú Hami, who are also Zagháï, or of the tribe of Sokai, are said by Mohammed Másíní, to dwell not only in the mountains near the western course of the Great River above Tomboktú, but also in the desert, mingled with the Tawárik, on the left bank of the same river below Kághó, and between that river and Sokkatú. And this information accords with the statement of Sultan Bello, who, speaking of the province of Kábi, west of Sokkatú, says, "its inhabitants, it is supposed, had their first father from Sanghee and their mother from Kashnah;" clearly implying by this genealogy, that the Zagháï, Sanghee, Sokai, or Benú Hami, have dwelt from time immemorial in Kábi, intermingled with and ruling the indigenous population.[61] The advance of the tribe or nation originally styled Tekrúr, from the vicinity of Jenni eastwards to Marra or Western Houssa, completely explains why Ibn Khaldún, placing the Ṣúṣú and then Málí next to Ghánah (an arrangement expressing historical perhaps rather than geographical relations), and beyond these Kághó, sets Tekrúr beyond, or, as he supposed, eastward from, the latter place; and also why Makrízí makes Tekrúr the western boundary of the great empire of Kánem or Bornú. In the last century Niebuhr the traveller learned that Tekrúr was the residence of a sultan, the vassal of Afnú (Houssa), who possessed Mara (Marra) and Adana (perhaps Ader).[62]

May not the pilgrimage on which Scott was led into the country of the Zachah (Edinb. Phil. Jour. IV. p. 49), have been directed to the tomb of one of the early apostles of Negroland, and to a consecrated spot of Tekrúr? Notwithstanding the intrinsic weakness of an argument founded on the resemblance of ill-written names, there is more of coincidence here than can be ascribed to accident. Near the site of Tekrúr, the first converted Negro state, is the town of Zághah, having a like reputation. The title Tekrúr is given to the Zagháï; the devotees of the desert direct their steps to the country of the Zachah at that part of the river; there also we find a country called Sanghee, a tribe named Sokai, and the Sungai language. It can hardly be denied that these names are related.

[61] Sultan Bello, in Denham, II. p. 452. From the Benú Hami of the tribe of Sokai, who live in the desert on the left bank of the river, the country of Sóghy, where Mungo Park was attacked (Clapperton, p. 334), obviously derived its name.

[62] Deutches Museum, 1790, cited by Walck. Rech. p. 73. Yakút, in his Geographical Dictionary, says, that the King of Kaúkaú made war upon the

Though the people of Ghánah always kept in view the original application of the name Tekrúr, even after the territory where it grew into importance became part of the empire of Málí, yet beyond the circle of exact local knowledge, such propriety of language was never thought of, and at a distance the name Tekrúr was employed in a very comprehensive and indefinite manner. Makrízí, in describing the pilgrimage of Mansá Músa, King of Málí, in A.D. 1324, styles him King of Tekrúr; but again, in the annals of A.D. 1351, he mentions another king of Tekrúr, who likewise passed through Egypt, and who certainly was not Mansá Suleïmán, at that time King of Málí. It is manifest therefore that Makrízí used the name Tekrúr in no properly restricted and perhaps in no fixed acceptation.[163] The Western Fellátah apply the epithet Tekrúrí to the religious classes of their own nation. In Egypt it is given generally to Mohammedan devotees, natives of Negroland; and when Sultan Bello makes Tekrúr comprise all Negroland from Dárfúr inclusively westward, he offers an example not of the correct use of that name, but of its widest abuse.[64]

The history of Tekrúr may be thus briefly recapitulated:—The Zenágah early established themselves on the Great River, above Lake Debú, where the continued tract of desert conducted them to its banks, and there founded the city of Zághah, from which they afterwards took their name. They embraced Mohammedism, nearly half a century before the Blacks in their neighbourhood, and thereby obtained a reputation of sanctity which was nowise diminished by their activity as slave hunters. The general conversion of Western Negroland compelling

---

Moslim of Ghánah on the west, and those of Tekrúr on the east. According to Ibn Sáíd (Hamaker, Specimen Cat. p. 209), Tekrúr, which thus appears to have been east (rather south-east) of Kaúkaú (Kághó), was also the western boundary of the Zagháï (of Zagháwah), or the empire of Kánem.

163 Not. et Extr. tom. XII. p. 637–8, note.

64 See *ante*, Note 69. Mollien (Voyage dans l'Intérieur de l'Afrique, I. p. 176) says, that in the Fellátah language, the word Toucolor signifies a Mohammedan priest. But he elsewhere (pp. 207, 215) seems to use that name as the designation not of a class but of a community. Toucolor, whence the Tucorones of De Barros, is an obvious corruption of Tokrúr.

them to go to a distance for their prey, they proceeded eastwards to Marra or Western Houssa, where the hilly region has been always, in an eminent degree, the country of slaves.[65] They thus broke the path in which they were afterwards followed by the people of Málí, and more recently still by the Fellátah. The kingdom of Tekrúr being extinguished in the west by the empire of Málí, rose more conspicuously in the east: though the people retained their old habitations, the political denomination completely shifted its place, and Tekrúr stood between Málí and Bornú. In the meantime the religious title Tekrúrí being widely usurped, the original and proper application of the name fell into neglect and oblivion.

KÚGHAH—KÁGHÓ—KAÚKAÚ—KARKAR.

Kúghah is said by El Bekrí to have been fifteen days from Ghánah; and if to this scanty information be added the statements of El Idrísí, that it stood on the Nile or Great River, and was nine days east of Samaḳanda, which was four days distant from Ghánah towards the south or south-east, it will be apparent that Kúghah was the place otherwise named Kághó. It was, of all the cities of the Blacks, that which furnished the largest quantity of gold,—the very remark made of Gago (Kághó) by Leo Africanus.[66] When Cadamosto relates

---

[65] The name Boushy (Baú-shi), now given to the hilly country south of Zegzeg, means the country of the Baúwa, that is, of the Slaves.

[66] Not. et Extr. p. 649. Leo (pt. VII. c. 7) says, that not above half or a third of the gold brought to Gago could find purchasers. Cowries were imported into Kúghah, and they were also the money of Gago. A Spanish writer (D. Jorge de Mendoza Dafranca) says of Muley Hamed,—"He increased his empire by the conquest of Gago and Tumbocotum, whence they bring an immense quantity of gold. And here I must state as a curious fact, that in the taking of Gago there was found, in that place, a piece of artillery, bearing the arms of Portugal; a small image of Our Lady, and a metal crucifix." (Papeles Curiosas, in the Egerton Collection, Brit. Mus. Additional MSS. No. 10,262, p. 235).

that, of the gold collected in Melli (Málí), part was sent to Oden (Waddán), part to Tombutto (Tomboktú), and the remainder to "a place called Cochia, which is the road to Syria and Cairo," it is manifest that he meant to speak of Kághó under the name of Kúghah.[167] But it has been shown that Kághó was also called Kaúkaú. It is therefore clearly ascertained that one place—the most important in Negroland—bore three different names,—viz. Kúgháh, Kaúkaú, and Kághó, of which the last alone was proper to it; the first two also designating, or appearing to designate, other places. But it is worth while to inquire more closely into the confusion arising from this frequent use of equivalent and equivocal names.

El Bekrí does not speak quite so concisely of Kaúkaú as of Kúghah: he enters a little into detail respecting the former place; he says that it was nine days from Tádmekkah, which was situate fifty days eastward from Ghánah, and forty from Ghodémis. Tádmekkah was evidently a Berber town, in the desert, while Kaúkaú was considered as belonging to Negroland; yet if we suppose Kaúkaú to have been south of Tádmekkah, or forty-nine days from Ghodémis, and little more than fifty from Ghánah, still it could not, within nine days of Tádmekkah, have been in Negroland properly so called, but only on its frontiers towards the desert. Indeed, it may be inferred from El Bekrí's words, that its inhabitants were of Berber rather than of Negro origin. They were called by the Arabs, he says, Bazarkáyín; they dressed *like the Blacks*, they worshipped idols *like the Blacks*, but their king was a Mohammedan. They always threw the remains of the King's dinner into the Nile,—an expression on which but little stress can be laid. El Bekrí, in tracing the course of the Great River eastwards from Ghánah, states that fourteen days below the latter place, it entered the territory of the Seghmárah; and "opposite to the Seghmárah," he adds, "on the other side of the river, is Kaúkaú." Now the Seghmárah also occupied the country north of Tádmekkah; they possessed therefore, or roved over, a desert exceeding a month's journey in extent. In so wide a

[167] Ramusio, 1554, tom. I. Navig. di Aluise Ca da Mosto, c. XIII.

compass, it conduces little to accuracy to learn that Kaúkaú stood opposite to them; and as to the river, it may have been the theoretical stream uniting the Nile of Ghánah with that of Egypt. It is plain enough that Kaúkaú, nine days from Tádmekkah, was a very different place from Kúghah on the Great River, fifteen days below Ghánah; but since Kúghah was also called Kaúkaú, it is not quite clear that El Bekrí has not confounded in some degree those two places, and ascribed to the one the characteristics of the other.[68]

In El Idrísí's accounts of Kúghah and Kaúkaú, there is nothing so remarkable as his tone of uncertainty and the doubts uttered by him. Thus he says of Kúghah, that "it stands on the northern bank of the Nile, the waters of which are drunk by its inhabitants. It belongs to Wanghárah, ***but some of the Blacks place it in Kánem.***" Again, he tells us that "Kaúkaú is the most celebrated city of Negroland: it is large, and stands on the banks of a river flowing through it from the north. ***But*** many of the Blacks affirm that this city is built on the sides of a canal; ***others say,*** on a river running into the Nile; but the more probable opinion is, that the river of Kaúkaú has a course of many days before it reaches that city, and is afterwards lost in the sands."[69] Doubts of this kind respecting the most important and celebrated cities of Negroland may be more naturally ascribed to ambiguity of information, than to actual want of it. Kúghah on the Great River below Ghánah, may have been confounded with Kaúghah adjoining Bornú, and thus transferred eastwards into the vicinity of Kánem. The celebrity of Kúghah (called also Kaúkaú) may have lent a semblance of importance to some place in the desert bearing apparently the latter name, and the physical geography of which was but little known.

Respecting the position of this Kaúkaú of the desert, our information is far from being satisfactory; yet it all points towards the desert fronting Houssa, or between that country and Aghades. East of Ghánah, and behind the Merásah, El Idrísí places the nomade tribe of the Beghámah. Between the

---

[68] Not. et Extr. p. 656.

[69] Jaubert's Idrísi, pp. 21, 22, 116.

Beghámah and the Azḳár who passed the summer on Ṭanṭanah, the range of hills bounding Fezzán on the south, was a distance of twenty days. Now from Kúghah to Kaúkaú, he tells us, was a journey of twenty days going ***northwards*** through the country of the Beghámah. It was the natural consequence of a system which arranged the frontier of Negroland in an undeviating straight line from west to east, to suppose that a route from Negroland to the desert went northwards: but, stripped of such inference, El Idrisí's statement amounts to this,—that Kaúkaú was twenty days distant from Kúghah, not in Negroland, but in the desert. Again, when speaking of Ṭanṭanah and the Azḳár, he says, "further south are Kaúkaú and the Demdem;" and then repeating the various opinions current respecting the river of Kaúkaú, he adds, "the country contiguous to this territory (Kaúkaú) on the east, is chiefly that of Kawwár, well known and much frequented." The well-known country of Kawwár lies half-way between Fezzán and Bornú, westward of which situation, and consequently in the desert, we must look for Kaúkaú. Obscure as these indications are in many respects, they are conclusive in showing that Kaúkaú, according to the Arab author's conception, was in the desert, between Kúghah and Kawwár, Ṭanṭanah and the country of the Demdem.[170]

Ibn Sáíd, who wrote in the latter half of the thirteenth century, or above a century later than El Idrísí, after stating that Kánem is the greatest kingdom of Negroland, that it has Fezzán on the north, and that it is the head of Bornú, adds, that it has on the west Kaúkaú, Bagharah or Tagharah, Tekrúr, &c. He says also, that "from Tádmekkah to Kaúkaú are ten stages, from Kaúkaú to Ghánah twenty; then follows the Ocean." The reduced distance here allowed between Tádmekkah and Ghánah, may have arisen from confounding the Kaúkaú of the desert with the city of the same name (called also Kúghah and Kághó) on the Great River. But on one point Ibn Sáíd speaks clearly, namely, that Kaúkaú was not comprised in the kingdom of Kánem, which then included

---

170 Jaubert's Idrísí, pp. 116, 117.

Bornú and part of the desert, but lay further west, between Tádmekkah and Ghánah.

Numerous as are the Arab writers of Geographical Treatises and Dictionaries, it is vain to seek in their pages for any information on so obscure a point as the position of Kaúkaú. They all copy preceding writers literally, particularly El Idrísí; and on opening their volumes, we are almost sure of reading, that "Kaúkaú stands on a river of the same name, coming from the north, and afterwards sinking in the sands of the desert, though some say," &c. Yet they present one striking variance; many, if not even a large majority of them write, not Kaúkaú, but Karkar. It may be said, indeed, that in Arabic writing, Kaúkaú is easily changed into Karkar, and that the latter name is probably only a clerical corruption of the former.[71] But can it be shown *à priori* that there could not have been a city or country named Karkar? and is not the readiness to suppose the corruption of Kaúkaú into Karkar, itself the result of a prejudice founded on the celebrity of the former of these names, and which was likely at all times to prompt copiers and compilers to a corruption of an opposite kind, namely, that of Karkar into Kaúkaú? Of two names resembling each other, the more famous and better known may be well presumed to have had the benefit of all doubts in the process of transcription; while on the other hand, if there were actually two important places named Kaúkaú in Negroland, it is inconceivable that Arab travellers visiting that region should have never called attention to so remarkable an instance of homonymy; nay, that Arab Geographers should never have even suspected the existence of two places of that name, but should have uniformly endeavoured to draw to a single point the double image before their eyes. The manifest double use of the name Kaúkaú; the remarkable absence of all direct testimony as to the existence of two places of that name; and the various

---

[71] Hartmann (Commentatio de Geogr. Afr. Edrísianâ, p. 43) says, that Ibnu-l Wardi alone has Karkar. But this is a hasty assertion. The Kitábu-l-járafíah, above cited, has also Karkar; and of four Geographical Dictionaries among the Arabic MSS. in the Library of the British Museum, viz., Nos. 7497, 7503, 7504, and 7505, the first three read Karkar. Ibnu-l Wardi sometimes writes Karkarah.

readings of geographers compiling from the same authorities, being maturely considered, it is impossible to avoid concluding, that there actually were not two places named Kaúkaú, but that there was in the desert a tract called Karkar, which Arab authors easily transformed into Kaúkaú. They separated this well-known name from the names Kúghah and Kághó, with which it had no apparent relationship, and set it on Karkar, wherewith it almost naturally coincided.[172]

But is there any direct and positive evidence, it will be asked, of the existence of a place or territory named Karkar? Yes, we reply, there is direct evidence to that effect, sufficient to confirm the authority of the numerous Arab geographers who write Karkar instead of Kaúkaú. Ibn Baṭúṭah informs us that the Desert of Káhir, eastward of Tekăddá, belonged to the Karkarí Sultan.[73] There is here no possibility of confusion; Kaúkaú, which that traveller had visited, was included in the empire of Málí; and Tekaddá, an independent state, stood between that place and Káhir, depending on the Karkarí. But Káhir had 'Ahír, the desert of the Tawárik, on the north and east; Tekaddá on the west; and southwards it extended—as we learn from Leo, who calls it Ghír—to the frontiers of Guber: in this latter direction, then, we may naturally look for the head quarters of the Karkarí.

A modern writer, who has collected much, but not always distinct information relating to the interior of Africa, after mentioning the Kadarko (probably the Kotú-n-kúra) and the Shaderbah (the river of Kábi), adds,—"some of these rivers open a communication with a tribe of heathens named Gargari, who live in tents, and are not black, but a red-skinned people, yet they are not of the Arabian stock. The best breeds of horses and mules come from these parts."[74] This is evi-

---

172 Kaúkaú كوكو in ordinary Arabic writing can hardly be distinguished from كركر, and the latter name is thus assumed to be the former.

73 Ibn Baṭúṭah writes "es-Sultan el-Karkarí," the latter word expressing not Sultan's dominion, but his native country or tribe.

74 Dupuis, in the passage referred to (Resid. in Ashantee, App. 55), says, that the Moslem merchants of Benin trade with the Gargari by means of those rivers. It is evident that he has here mistaken Bini, a name given by the people of Houssa to

dently a description of a Berber tribe, whose loose observance of the Mohammedan rites has caused them to be mistaken for pagans. They reared their horses and mules in the desert, and visited the high countries of Kachenah, Zamfarah, and Gúber, whence the rivers alluded to descend. Clapperton found the Tawárik near Kachenah to be in possession of a remarkably fine breed of horses. The same traveller learned that, five days south of Katagum there is an independent people named Kurrikurry, probably a colony of the Karkari who have fixed themselves on the eastern slopes of the hills of Baúshi.[75] In a route from Kanó to Tomboktú, described by an intelligent native of the former place, the following names occur in succession:—Berni-Kachenah (Berni means city), Berni-Gurgar, Zamfarah, Ulumdar, Mallay, Galefaty and Asben. Ulumdar is the name of one of the Arab tribes frequenting Houssa; Mallay means a town belonging to the indigenous population, or the Mallawa; Galefaty (Kiliwatí, in the Houssa language Kiliwawa) is the town of the Kiliwah, a Berber tribe; and Berni-Gurgar, on the frontier between Kachenah and Zamfarah, is probably the chief place of the Karkarí.[76]

The obscurity and indistinctness which hung over the most important place in Negroland being thus removed, there still remains the inquiry, whether Kúghah, Kaúkaú, or Kághó, still exists and flourishes; has it mouldered to decay, or does it still retain the pre-eminence which we know it to have held during at least six centuries? These questions, in the present state of our information, cannot be answered with perfect confidence. The brief journal of Amadi Fatouma, the only survivor of Park's second expedition, seems to contain no

---

the countries adjoining Núfí, and even to Bornú (Clapperton's Second Expedition p. 103), for Benin.

[75] Clapperton points out the situation of the Kurrikurry in the journal of his first expedition, II. p. 246. He speaks of the Tawárik horses in p. 317.

[76] About twenty years ago, M. Andrada, the Portuguese Minister in Brazil, collected much information from the natives of Houssa whom he found there in slavery. The most interesting portion of it was transmitted by M. Menézes de Drummond, to the Journal des Voyages, and afterwards appeared in the German periodical the Hertha, July 1827, whence it is here quoted.

mention of Kághó. But without the original of that journal, how can a critic decide peremptorily as to its contents? Is there nothing to awaken suspicion in the published translation of that journal; or is it not possible, nay even probable, that the name there read Kaffo was really Kághó? [177] Bowdich says, that the places passed on the river below Tomboktú are Uzzalin, Googara, Koolmanna, Gauw, &c. The last-named place is in Marra; Koolmanna is probably the Gourmon of Amadi Fatouma, in the kingdom of Ghurma; and Googara is Kúghah, the burr of the letter ghain being represented by an *r*.[78] Mohammed Másíní, in his description of the Kowára, places on its banks, ten days below Tomboktú, a city named Ghagró, which name, as we have neither the original document, nor an explanation of the translator's mode of representing the Arabic letters, we feel justified in supposing to be intended for Kághó.[79] Finally, in an account of the travels of an Egyptian-Arab, procured by Major Laing, are the following words:—"To the westward, between Houssa (Kachenah) and Yawoori [this is an indication of direction by the traveller in Núfí] is situated on the Niger, a town of immense magnitude and importance, called Kuku (Kaúkaú), of the power of which surrounding tribes stand in much awe." These allusions, taken together, seem to warrant the conclusion that Kúghah, Kághó, or Kaúkaú still exists and flourishes.[80]

The argument urged above to show that Kaúkaú is often written for Karkar may be thus briefly stated: Kaúkaú is described by Arab geographers with impossible conditions, the analysis of which shows that either there were two places named Kaúkaú, or two places not so named indeed, but of which the written names were so much alike, that, in nine cases out of ten, they would be both read Kaúkaú; and this is the preferable opinion. Having thus decided that the eastern Kaúkaú, or rather Karkar—as it shall be called hereafter for the sake of avoiding

[177] Park's Second Journey, 8vo. p. 288. In coarse Arabic manuscript, Kaffo would be hardly distinguishable from Kagho.

[78] Bowdich's Account of a Mission to Ashantee, p. 199.

[79] Clapperton's Second Journey, p. 330.

[80] Journal of Science, edited at the British Institution, vol. XIV. 1823, p. 8.

ambiguity—was the territory extending from the vicinity of the modern Aghades, to the frontiers of Gúber and Kachenah, we must now give a little attention to its river. Enough is known of Negroland in that quarter, to render it certain that a river described in such doubtful language, must belong to the desert. Streams flow southward from the mountains of Muḳsim near Aghades, and one of these was probably the river of Karkar.[81] Passing through this place, it turns westward (or rather south-westward), and then, according to some accounts, it winds towards the desert (or northward), and is lost in the sands. But some say that it joins the Nile (the Great River, or Kowára); and as the country north-west of the Quorrama is described as being well watered, and having rivers flowing through it to the Kowára, the river of Karkar may be assumed with probability to be one of them.[82]

LEMLEM.

Remrem—Demdem—Yemyem—Al-Límiyín.

"Going along the river," says El Bekrí, "westwards from Kaúkaú (Karkar), you come to the country of the Remrem (or Demdem), who eat all who fall into their hands." This sentence is copied verbatim by the greater number of the Arab geographers. El Idrísí however satisfies himself with merely stating that south of Ṭanṭanah are Kaúkaú (Karkar) and the Demdem; leaving it to be inferred that the last-named people are furthest south. From what has been said of the position of Karkar and the course of its river, it will be apparent that

---

[81] The rivers in 'Ahír on the northern side of Muḳsim (Walckenaer, Rech. p. 448) can hardly be supposed to flow southwards. But the Tatar merchant Wargee (Asiatic Journal, 1823, p. 16) also speaks of a great river one day's journey south of Aghades; though perhaps it was one of those rivers which have but a short existence after the rains (Walcknenaer, Rech. p. 450).

[82] Clapperton's Second Expedition, App. 332, 333.

the Demdem, being negroes and savages, must have been situate, not due west, but rather south-west of that place, and consequently must be sought in the hills of Kábi, facing the desert, and still inhabited at the present day by a wild and intractable race.[183]

In all accounts of Central Africa, from the time of El Bekrí to the present day, mention is made of cannibals variously called Remrem, Lemlem, Demdem, Yemyem, or N'yumn'yum. These names differ only in the consonants employed, one liquid being changed for another, except in the case of Demdem, which might be naturally an oral corruption of Remrem; if it be not merely a variety originating in error of transcription.[84] Are we then to believe that there are so many different nations of cannibals in Negroland, bearing names so singularly related to one another? Or is it not more likely that these various names are but modifications of one, which being the nickname of a particular class of savages, would be naturally carried about to the slave markets, and fashioned to suit the genius of every language which adopted it?[85] It is true that El Idrísí speaks of Lemlem and Demdem as of two distinct countries; but the position of his Lemlem depends on the westward course of the Great River to Ghaïárú, the absurdity of which has been already pointed out; and this error being corrected, his Lemlem and Demdem will be found to coincide.

---

[183] Not. et Extr. tom. XII. p. 655. Jaubert's Idrísí, p. 116.

[84] The *l* of the Arabs and *r* of the Africans so often displace each other, that the change of Lemlem into Remrem is quite regular. In Arabic writing Remrem is hardly distinguishable from Demdem, which might therefore have originated in the ambiguous characters of the former name. But it will be shown further on, that in Marra (adjoining the original Demdem) the *r* is often changed into *d*.

[85] It may be naturally presumed that the slave market, whence the designation first proceeded, was that of Ghánah, and therefore that its meaning should be found in the language of Tomboktú or territory of Ghánah. Now in that language *lemlem* signifies *to eat* (Caillié, tom. III. p. 311); and if the Kissúr be as simple in its construction as the Mandingo, it also signifies an *eater* or cannibal. Thus from *domo*, to eat, in Mandingo, comes the verbal noun *domo*, in the plural *domolu*, eaters —not man-eaters, as it is translated by Park (First Journey, p. 217), who writes *dummulo*—the name with which the Bambarans stigmatize their neighbours the Maniana.

In modern accounts of Negroland, frequent mention is made of a race of cannibals, styled Yemyem or N'yemn'yem; and every precise indication of them, from whatever quarter it may come, points to the same spot, namely the hilly country extending southward from Kanó.[86] The Yemyem of the present day, therefore, dwell at no great distance from the site of the Demdem of earlier ages. They occupy the remote continuation of the chain of mountains once inhabited by the latter: and if the changes necessarily effected in the northern part of that region, or Houssa, by the introduction of Mohammedism, the influx of Berbers, Zaghâï, and Fellátah, be duly considered, together with the fact that a wild people still keep possession of the hills on the frontier of the desert, it will appear a natural inference that the reproach of cannibalism, or the barbarity itself, has receded, owing to the progress of civilization, and that the Yemyem are the Demdem, changed in site and appellation only by the variations of the medium through which we view them.

If the Yemyem or N'yemn'yem of the present day be not

86 Burckhardt (Trav. in Nubia, p. 441) mentions the Yemyem without assigning their position. Einsiedel (Cuhn's Merkw. Reis. III. p. 436) vaguely connects them with Kanó. Hornemann (Trav. p. 119) sets them ten days south of the same place. Clapperton (Denh. and Clapp. Disc. II. p. 248) learned that the Baúwa in the country of Jacoba, between Kanó and Adamawa, are styled Yemyem; though Sultan Bello (Clapp. Sec. Exped. p. 250) removed the reproach of cannibalism to the country of Umburm, adjoining Jacoba. Hutchison also was informed in Ashantí (Bowdich's Mission, &c. p. 203), that the Yemyem are in Quollaliffa, and couples their name with that of Dall, a mountainous district, a few days south of Kanó. According to Abdu-r-Raḥmán Aga, the informant of Niebuhr (Deutches Museum, 1790), the Yemyem are in Adamawa. Again, Lander (Exped. to the Niger, III. p. 83) was told that the journey from Funda to Bornú might be accomplished in fifteen days, and that the only dangerous place on the road was the country of the Yemyem. Browne (Trav. in Afr. p. 356) and others who have gathered their information on the eastern side of the desert, speak of cannibals under the name of Gnumgnum (N'yemn'yem), in vague terms, not indicating their situation. But a Tatar merchant named Wargee, who visited Cape Coast in 1822, stated that the Namnam̃ (as he called them) were fifteen days south of Kanó, a distance reaching to the country of Jacoba. The ocular testimony of this intelligent man (Asiatic Journal, vol. XVI. p. 19), and of Sultan Bello, seems fully to establish the fact that cannibals exist in the quarter indicated.

the same people as the Lemlem, Remrem, or Demdem of early writers, it must then be inquired, What has become of these latter?[187] To deny such identity is to plunge back into obscurity: to suppose nations of negroes become extinct, or—a still bolder hypothesis—to have wholly changed their character. On the other hand, the supposition that the Baúwa (or Slaves) in the hills south of Kanó, to the remoter portion of whom the epithet Yemyem is now applied, once occupied the hills of Zamfara and Kábi, and were stigmatised as Demdem or cannibals, reconciles ancient with modern authorities; it attributes a just permanence to a great moral feature of Negroland, depending on peculiarity of race, modelled by physical circumstances; and it adjusts with remarkable precision the geographical elements involved in the question, assigning to the Demdem a position, which exactly coincides with that deduced from the statements connecting them with Karkar and the Great River. It may be assumed as certain, therefore, that the Demdem peopled the hills of the country now called Houssa.[88]

---

[187] It must not be supposed that Yemyem is the native name of any country or people south of Kanó: it is a foreign term applied with more or less vagueness to the inhabitants of that region. The misery and degradation of a people marked out especially as the prey of the slave hunter, exposes them to the imputation of cannibalism, which draws on them fresh injuries. Lander (Clapp. Second Exped. p. 292), on his way southwards from Kanó to Funda, saw at Fali-n-dúshi (the White rocks) for the first time, a people completely naked and ready to sell their offspring. But the natives of Zamfara also go nearly naked (Clapp. p. 178): the Kombori in Kotú-n-kúra, are still treated as Demdem (id. p. 146), and the pagan negroes near the desert (id. p. 334) are certainly not placed in circumstances more secure or favourable to civilization than the Baúwa further south. The change effected in Houssa by Mohammedism, and the influx of strangers, may be learned by comparing together the descriptions of that country by Clapperton and Leo Africanus. The latter writer (pt. VII. c. 11) knew of no city named Kachenah; the villages of the country so called were small and of the meanest construction; the people were of the deepest black, with noses and lips disproportionately large. He speaks of the people of Zamfara (c. 13) in still less flattering terms, concluding that "they are rather brutes than men."

[88] On the eastern side of the desert, the Shillúks are pointed out as a remarkably barbarous people, but yet they are not styled Yemyem. In the west, the people of

There is another name, much less known than Lemlem or Demdem, and apparently more comprehensive, applied to the inhabitants of the same region. Ibn Baṭúṭah says that Múlí, on the Great River, where the empire of Málí terminated, was in the country of the Límí (Al-Límiyín); and again, he says that Yúfí (Núfí) was in the country of the Límí; whence it is evident that the people so named were on the left bank of the river. The Blacks at Sofálah, he adds, were tattooed like the Límí of Genéwah, the latter name being in this instance used in the wide sense in which it was generally understood in the systematic geography of the Arabs. The practice of tattooing the body all over in fine patterns, is confined, in Central Africa, to the people of Marra. The Límí were said to wear clothing made of a plant called *worzi*, capable of resisting fire. The productions of their land seem to have been in general of a marvellous description.[89]

We are told that in the country of the Remrem or Demdem was a castle, whereon was a statue of a woman, adored

---

Bambara accuse their neighbours, the people of Maniana (the Manegnan of Caillié), of cannibalism, yet without applying to them the epithet Lemlem, Demdem, or Yemyem. From east to west there is but the one spot to which this name is constantly and distinctly given. With respect to the Manegnan (or rather Manegna, the nasal final being superfluous) it may be suspected that the imputation cast on them by their enemies has its origin in tradition, and that they are descendants of the Manes, reputed cannibals who overran the coast in the latter half of the fifteenth century.

[89] Al-Límiyín اللميين. This name occurs three or four times in Ibn Baṭúṭah's Narrative. M. Quatremère (Not. et Extr. 650) has read it Lâmes, in the unpointed Parisian MS. of El Bekrí. May not the Worzi be the Bordi (Walck. Rech. p. 448) of the Moors? Marmol (vol. I. fol. 31) quoting Ibn Gezzar, places the people called Lime (Límí) in Genéwah on the eastern side of the desert (that is, in the eastern part of the western division of the desert), between the cities of Rafin and Cuco. Rafin might be easily read for Rágha in Arabic text. Cuco is probably Kaúkaú or Kághó: it elsewhere occurs in the same author (vol. I. fol. 34, and II. fol. 221), but evidently referring to the place so named in the province of Algiers (Peyssonel et Desfontaines, Voy. dans la Régence d'Alger, &c., 1838, tom. I. p. 380). Marmol again places the Limin (Límiyín) (fol. 45) between the Zinj and Western Ocean, and calls them savages. All his hints combined show that they possessed the interior of Houssa.

by the people; and it is remarkable that in the traditions of Houssa the history of Zegzeg begins with the conquests of a female. It matters not that her name is Arabicised or her antiquity underrated by the native Chroniclers; they leave untouched the essence of the tradition, which is, that Zegzeg was founded by a heroine.[190]

NEGROLAND DIVIDED INTO NATIONS.

Ibn Khaldún, after making some prefatory remarks on the origin and genealogy of the Blacks, borrows from an earlier writer the following account of the nations into which they were supposed to be divided:—

"Ibn Sǻíd, a most diligent writer, enumerates nineteen nations of Blacks, beginning with the Zinj on the shores of the Indian Ocean, who have a city called Mombásah. They profess idolatry, and are the same people who in the reign of Al-Muǻtamid, seized on the city of Baṣrah; where great numbers of them were in slavery. They took up arms against their masters, and, assisted by the Zinj, got possession of the city.[91]

"Near the Zinj are the Berber, among whom Islamism

---

[190] Not. et Extr. p. 655. The founder of the state of Zegzeg, which includes Baúshí, was 'Amenáh, according to Bello (Denham's Disc. II. p. 450). Lander (Clapp. p. 290), who learned a different version of her history, says that she built a town called Almena. May not the remarkable rocks described by him, on the hill above that town, have given rise to the story of the statue?

[91] At the present day the servile and perhaps most numerous class of the population of the southern shores of the Persian Gulf, are Zinj, or Blacks, originally from Zinjibar (corrupted into Zanguebar), or the eastern coast of Africa. In Zinjibar, that is, the country of the Zinj, on the other hand, the rulers and upper classes are chiefly Arabs from 'Omán and the Persian Gulf. The tribe of the Lámí, who have given their name to Lámú, near Patta, are originally from the neighbourhood of Baṣrah. The event related in the text ceases to appear improbable when the nature and antiquity of the intercourse between Zinjibar and the Persian Gulf are considered.

made great progress. They have a city named Maḳdishó, which is partly inhabited by Mohammedan merchants. In their country are the people called Demádem, who go naked. It is recorded in history that these made an irruption into Abyssinia and Nubia, exactly at the time when the Tatars invaded Irak. After laying waste the country, however, they retreated homewards.[92]

"Adjoining the Berber are the Abyssinians, the most numerous and powerful of the Blacks. From their country Yemen once had its kings. The king of the Abyssinians was entitled Al-Negáshí, and the capital of his kingdom was the city of Kåber. The Abyssinians are Christians, but it is said that one of their kings embraced the true faith when Mohammed visited their country in the Hijra. They believe that they are destined to become masters of Yemen and all Arabia.[93]

"Next to the Abyssinians are the Bojá, a mixed nation of Christians and Mohammedans, who possess Suwákin, an island

---

92 The Berbers here spoken of are the inhabitants of the country called by the Greeks in general Βαρβαρία, and by the Arabs Al-åjemí—that is, foreign ; which latter name has been converted by ancient geographers into Azania (Ptolemy ; and Arrian, Perip. Mar. Eryth.), and by moderns into Ajan. The name Berber, in this as in most other instances, originated in the commercial and diplomatic language of the Roman Empire. The east-African Berbers are now called Somáli ; but their ancient designation still remains to Berberah, a town or rather encampment opposite to 'Aden. The tribe who possess Maḳdishó (the Magadoxa or Magadocia of our maps) are the Bajúna or Bagúna, called by the Sawáḥilí, or natives of the coast of Zinjibar, Wagúña. They are the Baẓúnah of El Idrísí (Jaubert's Idrísí, I. p. 55, where مدونه is read for بذونه). It will be shown further on, that the Demádem have been transferred to the eastern side of Africa by an ordinary effort of speculative geography.

93 The title of the Emperor of Abyssinia was Negusa Negast, or King of Kings. (Ludolf. Comment. p. 11.) The city called by the Arab writer Kåber was Ankó-ber (or the Pass of the Ankó, a tribe formerly occupying that tract, but now removed further north), at present the capital of Shoa. The Arabs and Abyssinians in ancient times were intimately connected. The language of Tigré, or Northern Abyssinia, is of Arabic origin, and even the Amharic is thought by Gesenius (Ersch and Gruber's Encyklopedie, art. Amharische sprache) to be an older offset of the same stock.

in the sea of As-Suweís (the Red Sea).[194] They have for neighbours the Nubians, who are brethren of the Zinj and Abyssinians, and have, on the west of the Nile, a city called Donḳalah. They are chiefly Christians, and border on Egypt, where many of them are sold as slaves. Adjoining them are the Zagháwah, who are Mohammedans, and from whom are sprung the Tájúah.[95]

" Next comes Al-Kánem, a populous kingdom, wherein the true faith is largely disseminated. Its capital city is Jíma. At one time the people of Kánem held the whole Ṣaḥrá in subjection; their ascendency being due to their intimacy with the Sultans of the house of Ḥafṣ, when this dynasty flourished in its prime.[96]

" Next to the people of Kánem, on the west, are the people of Kaúkaú, and after them Begh árah, and At-Tekrúr, and Kimi, and Yemyem, and Jábi, and Kúra, and Inkizár; by the side of the ocean towards the west they reach the people of Ghánah in the west. What precedes has been copied from Ibn Sáíd's work." [97]

---

[194] The Bojá or Bogá are the Βυγαείται of the Greek inscription of Axum, copied by Salt (Trav. p. 410). Under that general name was included all the tribes of the desert between Abyssinia and Egypt ; the Blemyes of ancient geographers, and the Bisharee or Bishareen of modern travellers.

[95] By the expression that the Nubians are brethren of the Zinj, it must be understood that they are of negro origin ; and indeed there is little reason to doubt that the Nubians on the Nile were originally a servile population, the progeny of the Nubah of Kordofán, who, in the course of events, became sole possessors of their master's domains. Their emancipation was forwarded by powerful external causes (see Edinb. Rev. No. 125. p. 297), and does not appear to have been accomplished by means of revolt or invasion, as was the case with the Zinj in Baṣrah, and the Funj in Sennár (Bruce's Trav. vol. VI. p. 370). When the Arabs conquered Nubia, they exacted an annual tribute of slaves, which was called *Bakt* (Quatremère, Mémoires sur la Nubie, II. p. 42), a word evidently derived from the ancient Egyptian language, in which *Bok* signified a slave.

[96] The family of Abú Ḥafṣ, of Berber origin, rose to the sovereign power in Tunis, in the early part of the thirteenth century. (Makrízí in Hamaker, Spec. Cat. p. 105.)

[97] The names of nations from Kaúkaú westwards, enumerated by Ibn Sáíd, are written as follows by Ibn Khaldún (MS. B.M. fol. 90) and Makrízí (Hamaker,

It is observable that the names in this list of places or countries lying west of Kánem (nine in number) are not recognized at all, or not confidently, by modern geographers. But before we proceed to determine the position of each of them, it will be advantageous to examine the information which Makrízí, in quoting Ibn Sáíd, adds to that of his author.[98] His words are as follows:—" Al-Kánem is an extensive region watered by the blessed Nile, and distant a ten days' journey from the borders of At-Tájú. In that country (Kánem) are naked Blacks, among whom are the Iklí, ruled by a just and mighty king; and Afnú, whose King, called Mastúr, guards his wives with extreme jealousy. Near this is another kingdom named Mambó, next to which lie Kátakúmá, Kátakú, and Ibkarem (Bekarmi), and another kingdom greater than the preceding, named Rábúmá (Umburm), the great kingdom of Haúdama (Adamawa), and the tribe of Ankarú, rich in herds, flocks, and elephants.[99] Next to these are the tribes Shádí, Mábiná,

---

Spec. Cat. &c. p. 107, whose orthography is here retained) respectively: ?agbárah نغارة I. K.; Baḳárah بقارة M.—At-Tekrúr التكرور I. K. & M.—Kimí كمي I. K.; Nama نمي M.—?emyem نميم I. K.; Temím تميم M.—Ḥáyí (?) حايي I. K.; Já جا M.—Kúra كورى I. K.; omitted by Makrízí.—Inkizár انكزار I. K. & M.

98 The comparison of texts made in the preceding note proves that Makrízí borrowed from Ibn Sáíd, but it is not easy to define the extent of his obligations to that writer. The Tunisian dynasty of Abú Hafṣ, the wars of the Zaghávah with the Wathekú (the opponents of that dynasty), and the invasion of Mábiná by the King of Kánem in 1252, referred to by Makrízí, all belong to the age of Ibn Sáíd, from whom he probably obtained his knowledge of them. But, on the other hand, Makrízí names the King of Kánem reigning in A.D. 1398, a century later than Ibn Sáíd. It appears more probable that his list of the Black nations near Kánem was the fruit of his own inquiry, than a transcript from an earlier writer.

99 As names changed from Arabic to European writing are apt to acquire thereby a more determinate form than properly belongs to them, those mentioned in the text shall be here represented in their original character, that the reader may be enabled to appreciate our conjectures respecting them. Iklí اكلي ; Afnú افنوا ; Mambó منبو. Caancouma (in Hamaker) كانكوما is evidently Kátakúmá كاتكوما wanting a point. In like manner Hamaker's Caancou must be changed

Abham, Atåná, Yáfalam, and Makabá, who are all naked Blacks, and hold clothed men in derision. The tribe of Mábiná is the most numerous, and the chief part of it is called Kálkín.[200] This region is covered with great trees and with pools from the overflowing of the Nile. It was invaded in the year 650 (A.D. 1252-3) by the King of Kánem, who killed many of the natives, or led them into slavery. Beyond this, westward to Kaúkaú, are many populous tribes, of which those next to Mábiná are the Adermá and Dafúmú, among whom are Mohammedan temples. Also the Abkalá (Ankalá), who have camels, wear skins for clothing, and are accounted unbelievers; and the Túkámá, who dwell on the borders of At-Tájú, possess palm-trees, and drink of the Nile. Al-Kánem is the greatest kingdom of Negroland, and has on the west Kaúkaú, then Baḳárah, Tekrúr, Nama, Temím, Já, and Inkizár, which extend in the west from the ocean to Ghánah." [1]

In this list of countries or tribes lying within the circle, as it were, of Kánem, the name Afnú, given by the people of Bornú to the adjacent part of Houssa, stands conspicuous, and cannot fail to be recognized. The Arab writer appears to have commenced his survey from a prominent point, the Iklí being probably on the frontier of Negroland, between Afnú and the desert.[2] Kátakúmá may also be fairly assumed to be the

---

into Kátakú. It may be thought that there is not sufficient authority to prove that Kátakúmá and Kátakú are distinct countries. But Burckhardt (Trav. in Nubia, p. 433) has stated the position of the latter, and the districts comprised in it (nearly all pointed out by Denham) with so much precision, that his testimony, corroborated by that of Mohammed Miṣrí (Journ. of the Roy. Inst.), decisively separates Kátakú from the Katagum (Kátakúmá), which was visited by Clapperton.—Ibkarem ابقرم —Rábúmá رابوما —Haúdama هودمي —Ankarar انكرر is probably written by an error of the pen for Ankarú انكرو.

[200] Shádí شادي ; Mábiná مابنا ; Abham ابهم ; Atåná اتعنا ; Yáfalam يافلم ; Mekba مكبا ; Kálkín كالكين.

[1] Aderma ادرما ; Dafúmú دفومو ; Abkalá ابكلا we have ventured to change into Ankalá انكلا ; Túkámá توكاما.

[2] Afnú is the name given by the people of Bornú to Houssa (Lucas in Proc.

Katagum of Clapperton; the writer therefore proceeds eastwards or south-eastwards, and consequently Mambó or Manbú will be near the country called Anbur by the English traveller. Continuing in the same course, he necessarily arrives at Kátakú and Bekarmi, having thus traced the frontiers of the independent tribes of Bornú facing Kánem.[3] He then seems to make the tour of the hilly country forming the remote boundary of the same region; but, it must be confessed, that this portion of his path is less easily investigated, and leaves a larger scope to conjecture. However it is a natural supposition that he enumerates the chief nations or tribes behind the line already traced, and so, eastward from Bekarmi, are Rábúmá (Umburm, a kingdom near Jacoba), Haúdama ('Adám, or, in the language of Houssa, Adamawa), and Ankarú (Angarú), the western part of Bornú.[4]

Afr. Assoc. I. p. 165), or the eastern part of it. Einsiedel (Cuhn's Merkw. Reisen. III. p. 439) understood that Hafnou (Afnú) lies between Bornú and Zegzeg. Abdu-r-Rahmán Aga, Niebuhr's informant (Walck. Rech. p. 72) also uses the name Afnú as equivalent to Houssa. The Sultan of Tekrúr, he says, who possessed Mara (Marra), was tributary to the Sultan of Afnú, residing in Zamfara. Seetzen also (Von Zach's Monatliche Correspondenz, vol. XXI. 1810, p. 152), places Affano immediately to the west of Bornú. See also the Bulletin de la Soc. de Geogr. de Paris, tom. VI. p. 169, where Kachenah is stated to be the capital of Afnú. It is remarkable that in Bornú, and the adjoining deserts, the Arabic expression Súdán (country of the Blacks) is always given to Afnú or Houssa (Lucas, as above; Denham's Discoveries, &c. II. p. 85), a strong proof that it was the country of the Remrem or Demdem, and the point to which the slave merchants directed their march.

[3] Kátakú comprises Mandara, Musgow, and the other provinces on the west of the River Shary, which are therefore not named. It is not to be ascribed to mere chance, that two names are changed, by the addition of a single point to each, into Kátakúmá (the Katagum of Clapperton) and Kátakú, the Katákó of Burckhardt, the Kotoko of the native of Bornú cited in the preceding note (Bullet. Soc. Geogr.), and the Kotko of Seetzen (p. 153).

[4] Umburm is in the country of the Yemyem near Jacoba (Clapp. Sec. Exped. p. 250). In Sultan Bello's account of Baúshí (Denham and Clapp. Disc. II. p. 451), he mentions a province of that country called Aádám. We cannot venture to say whether this is the root from which Adamawa is derived, but it might be easily changed in discourse into Haúdama. Angarú (Ankarú) is three long days'

Adjoining these, we should expect to find Baúshí, with its decried inhabitants; and accordingly our author here names several tribes of savages "who hold clothed men in derision." Shádí is certainly the name of a place in Baúshí; but we must not yield to the temptation of detecting resemblances of names which may easily prove deceitful.[205] It is more important to consider the force of the words "from Mábiná westwards to Kaúkaú," from which it may be concluded that Mábiná lay towards Kaúkaú, or was the north-westernmost point of the region described, and consequently that the Arab author proceeds in a circle, agreeably to our hypothesis, and terminates at a point in Afnú whence he first started. His picture, too, of a region covered with great trees and pools from the overflowing of the Nile, corresponds exactly with the physical character of Zegzeg and Zamfara.[6] The invasion by the King of Kánem for the purpose of carrying off slaves, further confirms the supposition that the country described was Houssa and Baúshí. What other region had equal attractions for the slave hunter,—or where else could be found a long line of savage tribes extending to the frontiers of the desert and of Kaúkaú? Next to the Mábiná, towards the desert, followed the Adermá

---

journey west of the capital of Bornú (Mohammed Mísrí, in Jour. Roy. Inst.), and within the dominions of Bello (Clapp. in Denh. Disc. II. p. 313). It is the Ungura of Hornemann, which was supposed to be identical with Wanghárah (Proc. of Afr. Assoc. II. p. 200).

205 One of the natives of Houssa, interrogated by M. Menézes de Drummond (Hertha, July, 1827, p. 12), mentioned the Schadŭh (Shádí) among the tribes depending on Zegzeg. Can the name Mábiná be the same word as Foobina, said by Mohammed Másíni (Clapp. Sec. Exped. p. 335) to be sometimes affixed to Adamawa? The name Bobyra, given in the Quarterly Review (No. 77, p. 178), on the authority of Clapperton, in whose published Journal it nowhere occurs, might easily have its origin in Fobina, or even Mabina ill-written in Arabic. According to Abdu-r-Rahmán Aga, the King of Tekrúr possessed Marra and Adana. One of the Itineraries collected by Dupuis (Resid. in Ashantee, App. p. 129,) places an Etana on the river west of Marra.

6 Clapperton found the plains of Zamfara covered with a chain of lakes which are connected in the rainy season; and Lyon (Trav. in N. Afr. p. 151) was told that the country between Kanó and Zegzeg is annually covered with water.

and Dafúmú, who were not strangers to the Mohammedan rites; and then came the Túkámá (Togáma) and Angála, of whom the former have given their name to a place in the desert not far from Kachenah, while similar traces of the latter remain on the shores of Lake Chad.[7] The Túkáma of Makrízí, it is true, were on the east of Kánem, near Tajúah; but so easily do the tribes of the desert change their dwellings, that there is no improbability in the supposition that the same tribe subsequently spread westwards and settled near Houssa.

In considering the interpretation here offered of Makrízí's statement, less weight is to be allowed to the resemblance of names than to the order, coherence, and accordance with probability which the whole passage acquires from the mode of viewing it. Some points in it may be obscure; but others, as Afnú and Katagum, hardly admit of doubt; and we feel justified, therefore, in concluding that the nations or countries, as Kaúkaú, Baḳárah, Tekrúr, &c., which Makrízí (copying Ibn Såíd) arranges west of Kánem, are all excluded from the region above described—that is to say, from Bornú and the hills of Baúshí and Houssa immediately encompassing it on the west.

In endeavouring to ascertain the positions of the various nations mentioned by early Arab writers as extending across Negroland, it will be advantageous to compare the whole series of those nations with the list of kingdoms arranged by Leo Africanus in the same line. For this purpose Ibn Såíd's list shall be inverted, or taken from west to east; and then the names which are clearly related being placed opposite to each other, we shall have the geography of Negroland in the latter half of the thirteenth century, contrasted with that of the beginning of the sixteenth, as in the following table:—

---

[7] The name Angalawha, occurring on the northern shores of Lake Chad, is easily traced by an analogy of the Bornowí language indicated by Denham (the tree Kuka being called also Kukawha,) to Angala, which name also occurs on the southern shores of the lake. The town or station of Togáma is seven days distant from Kachenah, on the road to Aghades (Lyon's Trav. p. 131). Hornemann (Proc. Afr. Assoc. II. p. 300) gives some account of the tribe so called.

Ibn Sáíd.	Leo.
Ghánah	Gualata.
	Ghinea.
	Melli.
Inkizár	Tombuto. Gago.
	Guber.
Kúra.	
	Agadez.
Jábí.	
	Cano.
Yemyem.	
	Casena.
Kimí.	
	Zegzeg.
Tekrúr.	
	Zanfara.
Bagharah.	
	Guangara.
Kaúkaú.	
Kánem	Borno.
	Gaoga.
Zagháwah.	
Núbah	Nubia.

Here then, in the first place, it it manifest that Ghánah coincides with Gualata (Walata). The salient point of Negroland towards the north-west ranks as the extreme west, and the countries which lie to the south, though extending further westward, are placed after it. Hence the Ghinea and Melli of Leo, both supposed by him to reach the ocean, nevertheless follow Gualata.

From the southern countries, Ghinea and Melli, Leo turns eastwards down the river to Tombuto and Gago; and thence proceeds across the desert to Guber, on the northern frontiers of Houssa. Ibn Sáíd, on the other hand, goes in two steps from Ghánah to Kúra, the western frontier (as will be seen further on) of the same region. He seems to take the straight road through Negroland to the eastern settlements of the Tekrúrí, while Leo keeps to the desert and the roads frequented by Moorish merchants. Inkizár then appears to be the region encompassed by the great circuit of the river between Jenni and Kághó. Its collective name, little known to geographers, probably never enjoyed political importance, but it seems still to survive in the name of the language called by Caillié the Kissour. This language extends from Jenni down the river to Tomboktú, where it is spoken, as the same traveller informs us, by the negro or indigenous population. But there is no authority for supposing that it extends no further eastward than Tomboktú; and it seems more reasonable to enlarge the limits of a language occupying so important a position, so that it may fill the area encircled by the river, and comprise Kághó (the Gago of Leo) in its domain. Inkizár then was a kingdom situate on the right bank of the Great River, between Jenni, Tomboktú, and Kághó, of which the political fabric has long since fallen to ruin, while a vestige of the original bond of unity still remains in the Kissour language.[208]

From Gago Leo passes to Guber, on the northern frontier of Houssa; then to Agadez, which is more easterly; then to Cano and Casena, lying further south; then to Zegzeg and Zanfara, still more in the rear, till at length he arrives at Guangara (Wanghárah), which fills the remote interior. But he shows his imperfect acquaintance with Houssa, by setting Casena (Kachenah) on the east of Cano (Kanó), and Zanfara in like manner on the east of Zegzeg. It is not surprising, therefore, that he should place Guangara on the east of Zanfara. He may possibly have confounded (like some modern writers) Angarú, the western province of Bornú, with Wan-

---

[208] If we suppose the word Kissour pronounced N'Kissúr with the nasal sound, which among the Africans so often precedes the letter *k*, then its affinity with Inkizár becomes more apparent. The Portuguese, like the Arabs, employ an initial vowel in prefixing the nasal; thus for N'Yáka, N'Yambána, N'Góla, they write Inhaqua, Inhambana, Angola. Of the guttural pronunciation which seems to foreign ears to confound the *a* and *u*, many examples might be given. Leo Africanus says that one language (which he calls Sungai) extended from Málí to Kághó; and as we know that the Kissour, commencing at Jenni, now extends at least to Tomboktú, we are justified in concluding that it is the Sungai, or the language to which the Zagháï, the chief inhabitants of Inkizár, lent their name. We have seen that the word Dakno, the name of the ordinary beverage of the people from Jenni downwards, was in use below Tomboktú in the fourteenth century. (See above, p. 84.) It avails little against this, that the Sungai language was also spoken in Málí: for what is more natural than that the language of the most populous and industrious part of an empire should be generally spoken in its capital; and that a Moorish merchant should give little attention to the language of the lower classes?

ghárah or Guangara; but it is more likely that his information was substantially good, and that he knew Wanghárah to be a region extending widely at some distance from Houssa; but his systematical ideas left no room for such expansion south-westward from Houssa, and consequently he was obliged to shift Wanghárah to the south-east. Since Nufí and the other comparatively industrious countries on the Great River, are not expressly named by him, it may be fairly presumed that they were included in his Wanghárah.[209]

Ibn Sáíd, in like manner, passes from Inkizár to Houssa; not however to the northern part of this country next to the desert, but to its western side near the river. He goes not in the track of the merchant or slave dealer, but in that of the slave hunter. It may appear indeed difficult at first sight to recognize any part of Houssa in the names Kúra, Jábí, &c., but a little patient examination will dissipate the obscurity which involves them, and concentrate on them so many rays of probability as to guide us safely through the difficulties encompassing the first steps of our inquiry.

In the Geographical Dictionary of Yakút, an earlier writer than Ibn Sáíd, and who is copied with little change by Abú-l-fedá, the names Kúra and Jábí occur together, with such explanatory details as to prove that the former is applied to the river Kowára, while the latter (probably pronounced

[209] Two intelligent natives of Kanó, who were in London a few years ago, when interrogated respecting Wanghárah, agreed in stating that it is "behind Ako," or Yariba. In the same vague manner probably, Leo Africanus, little acquainted with the interior, conceived it to be behind Zamfara. But his description of Wanghárah (pt. VII. c. 14), the nature of the journey to it, its trade, and its fear of Tomboktú, leave no doubt as to the country intended by him. The meditated invasion of Wanghárah by the King of Bornú, may indeed provoke scepticism; but let it be considered that the historical traditions related to Clapperton (Second Exped. p. 102, 103) by the King of Boussa (Busá), testify the former conquests of Bornú on the western side of the Kowára. Leo had a very inadequate idea of the extent of Negroland south of the Great River. He even speaks of the ocean encircling the desert from Cape Nún to Gaoga (pt. I. c. 2). He could not, consistently with such views, place the distant and populous country of Wanghárah south-westwards from Zamfara.

Gábí) seems meant for Kábí. It is there stated that the King of Kaúkaú (Kághó) wages war with the moslim of Ghánah on the west, and with those of Tekrúr on the east; and that a little to the east of Kaúkaú is the Lake Kúra, which must consequently be near Tekrúr: and, indeed, the author adds, that it is navigated by the Tekrúri and their neighbours dwelling on its northern bank. On the shores of this lake is Jábí, near the capital of which flows the Nile of Ghánah, so that the continuity of the Nile of Ghánah with Lake Kúra seems to be here offered as a fact; and this statement must not be set in the same category with the theory afterwards enunciated by the Arab geographer, that Lake Kúra is the common source from which issue the Niles of Ghánah, of Egypt, and of Makdishó.[10]

The same authors inform us that the tribes inhabiting the countries near Lake Kúra were cannibals: among the people of Jábí, whoever died was eaten by his neighbours. No one had ever seen the south side of the lake, but it was known that, at its remote end, it branched into two; and that by some means it extended westward into Kánem, whence flowed the Nile of Egypt. Now at the present day, the Kowára is generally called by the natives a lake; its name, written by them, is Lake Kúra; it

---

[10] Ibn Sáíd died A.D. 1286, at an advanced age. Yakút, of whose Geographical Dictionary the Bodleian Library possesses a copy, flourished somewhat earlier. Both these writers are quoted by Abú-l-fedá, who died A.D. 1331. Yakút and Abú-l-fedá cite Ibn Fátimah with no other variance than is usual in different MS. copies of the same work. The Jábí of Abú-l-fedá is clearly preferable to Yákút's Hání (see Note 197); but the Bedí of the former and the Yuthí of the latter are probably equally erroneous. It may seem a bold emendation to alter them into Yúfí or Núfí; but let it be considered that the country now called Núfí or Niffí may have changed its name with its population; that Ibn Batútah clearly means Núfí when he speaks of Yúfí; and that the name written Yúfí in the Gayangos MS., is in other MSS. written Yuwí (Lee and Kosegarten, Lee's Ibn Batútah, p. 238), and in others Buwí (Burckhardt, Trav. in Nubia, p. 491; and Lee). Now Bedí بدي and Yuthí يذي lie, with respect to Buwí بوي, Yúwí يوي and Yúfí يوفي, within what may be called reasonable limits of corruption, and the proposed change brings all into order.

is thought by them to join the sea, or rather to become a sea, a little below Núfí; they are quite ignorant of its southern termination, but know that it separates into what they consider as two branches, by one of which (the Chadda) it is supposed to communicate with Lake Chad, in Kánem and Bornú, and thence to mingle its waters with those of the Egyptian Nile.[211] In the country adjoining the Kowára and the Chadda are still found the Yemyem or cannibals. Thus it appears that the rudiments of the geographical system of the thirteenth century, so far as regards the waters of Central Africa, were precisely the same which now compose the native accounts of the Kowára, and its supposed continuation, the Chadda.[12]

Next to Jábí, in the east, Ibn Sáíd places Yemyem, then Kimi, of which we are unable to give any account. Next to that, and towards the north perhaps, he sets Tekrúr; then Bagharah, probably a tribe of the desert, and then Kaúkaú,

---

[211] Abú-l-fedá and Yakut wrote Kúra كُورَى; in one of the Routes (No. 4) published by Dupuis the river is called Koara كُورَا, though had the points been correctly written, we should probably have had Kúrá. Bello writes in his map Kowára كوَار, or, as our travellers have called it, Quorra. In Brahima's Itinerary (Bowdich, Mission, &c. p. 491), and in another translated by De Sacy, (Walck. Rech. p. 453), the Great River is named Lake Koad or Caudh كوض, which ought rather to be read Kúḍa. Further on we shall show that in these Itineraries the Arabic letter Dád ض is substituted for *r*; so that Lake Kúra is here intended. The Kowára, Kúra, or Quorra is frequently styled by the natives a sea or lake, according to some accounts, of forty-eight days' sail in extent (Ali Bey Badia's Travels, I. p. 338). Clapperton (Denham, Disc. II. p. 269) was told that the river Kowára falls into the sea (of Nyffi or Núfí) at Raka, where it is as wide as from Kano to Katagum, or about 150 miles. But not to multiply authorities, it will be sufficient to observe that Sultan Bello believed Raka (Rághá), —which has been recently reached by Mr. Jamieson's steamer Ethiope,—to be a sea-port, and represented it as such in his letter to the King of England.

[12] According to Ibn Fáṭimah, "when any one among these people dies, they cast the dead body to their neighbours, and their neighbours do the like for them." So Sultan Bello related (Clapp. Sec. Exped. p. 251) that in Umburm, where those who ail are killed at once, for economy, "the person falling sick is requested by some other family, and repaid when they have a sick relation."

after which comes Kánem.[13] Leo, on the other hand, passes from Guangara (Wanghárah) eastwards to Bornú, which coincides sufficiently well with the Kánem of Ibn Sáíd to serve with it as an established point of adjustment. He then goes to Gaoga, a kingdom extending, according to him, from Bornú to Nubia, and which appears to be the Kaúghah placed by some modern inquirers in the Baḥr el-Gazel. At all events care must be taken not to confound the Kaúkaú of Ibn Sáíd, which lay beyond the north-western bounds of Kánem and Bornú, with the Kaughah of Leo, on the east of the latter kingdom.[14] East of Kánem stands Zaghâwah in Ibn Sáíd's

---

[13] Kimí might without much violence be changed into Límí, and thus explain the name Al-Límiyín. At-Tekrúr we may assign, on the authority of Abdu-r-Raḥmán Aga, to Marra, which probably extended from Zamfara westwards between Guber and Kábí. The Bagh́árah or Baḳárah were probably a tribe of the desert. The Kaúkaú of Ibn Sáíd is too far east to be the city of that name on the Great River; we must suppose him therefore to extend this name to Karkar.

[14] Leo's Gago seems to be identical with the Caugha of Hornemann, or Kaúka of Burckhardt (Trav. in Nubia, p. 436). Its empire extended, he says, from Bornú to Nubia. The use of the name Bornú, in former times, however, and the modern geography of the countries round Lake Chad, are involved in an obscurity which it does not lie within the scope of this essay to dispel. Leo's text offers not only the names Gago and Gaoga, but also, in two instances, Gaogao. He says (pt. VII. c. 14), that while he was in Negroland, the King of Bornú marched against Wanghárah; but learning, on his way, that Omar, King of Gaogao, meditated an attack on his dominions, he turned back, and Wanghárah was saved. But, in this passage, Gaogao is a misprint for Gaoga, as Leo himself discloses by naming the King of Gaoga "Omar chi oggidí regna." In the other instance (pt. VII. c. 1), his Gaogao is justly changed by Marmol (vol. III. fol. 21) into Gaoga. Leo (pt. I. c. 7) having enumerated the fifteen kingdoms of Negroland visited by him, adds, that there are three times as many, sufficiently well known, lying to the south of the preceding; and names five of them, viz. Bito, Temiam, Dauma, Medra, Goran. Marmol (vol. I. fol. 15), in copying this passage, omits Dauma, and substitutes for it Mandinga. But Leo had no idea of increasing the kingdoms of Western Negroland. His Bito is the Bede of Denham and Clapperton, adjoining or comprised in the modern Bornú. Einsiedel names together, Schikou—the Schaïkou of Lyon (Trav. in N. Afr. p. 126), two days from the capital of Bornú—Bitou (Leo's Bito), and Engar (Angarú). Temiam may be an error for Yemyem: Dauma is probably the Doma of our maps, or the country on the right bank of the River Chadda. Medra seems to

list, and beyond that Núbah, which coincides with Leo's Nubia.

The results obtained by comparing Ibn Sáíd's list of Negro nations with that furnished by Leo, are not, in a general view, of a doubtful character. At the extreme west, the coincidence of Ghánah with Walata is manifest. It is hardly less certain that Inkizár is the country embraced by the Great River, between Jenni and Kághó, and in which the Kissour (perhaps rather N'Kiṣár) language prevails. Though the Kánem of Ibn Sáíd and the Bornú of Leo do not exactly coincide, yet they approach so nearly to coincidence as to serve for terms of adjustment in the compared schemes. The tracts extending therefore between Inkizár and Kánem, in the one author, and from Gago to Bornú, in the other, may be said to lie between the same meridians, and to contain either the same countries under different names, or contiguous and intermingled countries. Now within those limits Leo describes the greater part of Houssa, proceeding, or meaning to proceed, from west to east, and from north to south. Ibn Sáíd, commencing with Kúra, goes on to Tekrúr and Kaúkaú, evidently from west to east, and from south to north. Tekrúr extended westwards from Zamfara (which may indeed have been included in it) to the desert, and therefore Kúra, Jábí or Gábí, Yemyem and Kimí, were all south-westward of the countries of Houssa named by Leo.[215] There can be little doubt that Kúra was

be Mandara, one letter being obliterated in the Arabic MS. Goran (in Marmol Gorhan), which is often referred to by Leo, is evidently the Desert of Kordofán. This name كردفان might easily become, in negligent writing, Korhán كرهان ; or as Leo, uniformly writing *kef* with a *g*, and omitting the aspirates, would represent it, Goran. Another region often named by Leo, may be fitly considered here. In the Desert of Seu, south of Bornú (pt. VII. c. 15), and environing an immense lake (pt. I. c. 27), called the Lake of the Desert of Gaoga (pt. I. c. 2), he places the sources of the Niger (pt. I. c. 3). It is obvious that the lake alluded to is Lake Chad, and that the name Seu is the root of the appellative Showy, and the name Shouaa, respectively given by Denham to a town on the Shary, and the Arab tribes inhabiting the adjacent country.

215 Yakút and Abú-l-fedá both mention the towns of Maghzá and Jájah in the vicinity of Lake Kúra. Al-Maghzá, according to the former writer, was the port in which were fitted out the fleets of the King of Tekrúr, "who wages perpetual war

a district situate on the Great River, the name of which is variously written or pronounced Kúra, Kuḍa, Quorra or Quolla. Jábí was Kábí, to the east (or south-east) of which lay Yowí or Yúfí (the modern Núfí), on the northern shore of Lake Kúra, and under which, as we are also informed, flowed the Nile of Ghánah.[16]

The difference between Ibn Sáíd and Leo in their modes of viewing the same region, may be naturally ascribed to changes in the channels and manner of intercourse with it. The people of Gúber once possessed the desert of 'Ahír, but were displaced by the Tawárik. The invasion of Tekaddá by the people of Málí, had probably for its object to relieve the trade of Kághó from the exactions levied on caravans in the desert. It can hardly have failed to improve the road through that country, and increase the influx of strangers. A few years later,

with the infidels to the south of his states." Al-Maghzá signifies the place whence invaders sally forth. Abú-l-fedá however differs from Yaḳút in assigning both Maghzá and Jájah, not to Tekrúr, but to Kánem. Jájah (perhaps the Gagai of Clapperton, Sec. Exped. p. 174) was the capital of a petty state situate probably between those two kingdoms. It was remarkable for its fertility and variety of its productions; among other things for its spotted sheep (described by Lander in Clapp. Sec. Exped. p. 259–60). But it must be observed that the Arab geographers, in describing the bearings of those places, particularly in reference to the lake, speak in general the language of misconception.

16 Bowdich remarks (Mission to Ashantee, p. 478 note), that the name of the river written Kúra, Kúda, &c. was always pronounced Quolla by the natives in their conversations with Mr. Hutchinson. Ignaz Pallme (in the Athenæum, 1840, p. 54), a traveller in Kordofán, relates that the natives of that country think that the Bahr el-Abiad may be followed westward through Baghermi, Kúḳo (Kouka), and Niero (Naroo, the hilly country north-east of Zegzeg); and "further on (he says), in Kúla (Kúra) flows a river not identified" (that is, different from the Nile). Browne also (Travels in Africa, p. 254) heard in Darfúr of Darkulla (the Land of Kúla or Kúra), where pepper was in abundance, and the rivers were navigated in large canoes. He indeed supposed Darkulla to lie towards the south. But his map exposes his mistake; for the rivers Bahr Wullad Ráshid, B. el Salamat, and B. Heimad, crossed on the route to Darkulla, and which he places to the south and west of Baghermi, bear the names of Arab tribes dwelling in Wadaí and on the shores of Lake Chad (Burckhardt, Trav. in Nubia, pp. 433, 436). The route therefore went westwards.

Aghades was founded, probably by the Kiliwah (the Kolluvi of Hornemann), who are now the predominant Berber tribe on the frontiers of Houssa. When these various changes are all taken into consideration, it will no longer appear surprising, that while Ibn Sáïd viewed Houssa from the road opened to it by the people of Tekrúr, Leo should look at it only from the opposite quarter, or from Aghades.[217]

It is needless to follow the parallel between the systems of Ibn Sáïd and Leo beyond the western frontiers of Kánem and Bornú. Further east, the few points touched on by Arab geographers are not liable to misinterpretation. The inquiry into the early geography of Negroland, so far as concerns representations founded on fact, might here terminate. But it is worth while to observe how the framers of theories, the compilers of Dictionaries and Complete Treatises of Geography, dealt with the obscurer portion of it: how they endeavoured to fill up every void, and by arbitrary suppositions to give unity and coherence to their fragmentary information. The popular belief that the Great River of Negroland unites with the Nile of Egypt, is of ancient date, and may perhaps be traced back even to the time of Herodotus. It is stated with more or less distinctness by all the Arab geographers. Leo, however, discarded it, and adopted an original opinion of his own. The Shary, according to him, is the source of the Niger; for this river, he says, rises in the Desert of Seu (or country of the Shaúá), south-east of Bornú, and enters the

[217] The Kiliwah (the Kalawa of Capt. Lyon, Kolluvi of Hornemann), a Tawárik tribe, are masters of Asben, or the territory between Houssa and Aghades. Their town in Guber is called by Clapperton Killiwawa or Calawawa, by the Tatar merchant Wargee, Galibaba. Clapperton frequently mentions also the Kilghí (whom he calls Killgris), another powerful tribe of the same nation. Their territory is the kingdom called by Bowdich (p. 208), Kallaghee, fourteen days' journey from Gamhadi (Kambari), or from the Quolla, crossing the Gambarou (Kamba-róa, or Kamba water) on the tenth. Kamba is apparently the name given by the indigenous population to Kábi, or a part of Yaúrí (Dupuis, Append. 85). The Gambarou of Bowdich is the Gulbi Kambáji, or river of Kambáji or Konbash of Dupuis' Itineraries (App. 126 and 192). The name Kilghí is changed by the Blacks into Kilinghi (see Note 158), whence comes the title Kilinghiwa given to the King of Kachenah (Walck. Rech. p. 451).

Lake of Gaoga (the Chad). Respecting the hypothetical course of the river westwards from the lake, he is quite silent; and when he says that Cano is 500 miles east of the Niger, he seems to acknowledge his ignorance of its course south of that country. However, he believed it to flow westwards by Tomboktú and Jenni to the Western Ocean.

At the present day all African geographers believe in the junction of the Kowára with Lake Chad. Some suppose the line of connexion to be formed by the Quorrama and the Yeou; others look upon the Chadda as the continuation of the Kowára, and think that they can trace its course into Lake Chad by the river of Katagum and the Yeou; while others again carry it through Adamawa into the Shary.[18] All this hypothesis arises naturally from the constitution of the human mind, which is averse from doubt and systematic suspension of opinion. It hurries on to the solution of every problem presented to it. Furnished with a knowledge of portions of seas, continents, or rivers, it feels no pleasure in devising their limits and separations, but prefers joining the fragments together, as if it thus advanced a step in discovery, or mounted to a higher and simpler truth. Illustrations of this remark might be drawn from the history of geography in every age and country. It is not extraordinary therefore that Yaḳút, copied by Abú-l-fedá and others, should delineate decisively and with the air of a master, that assemblage of waters in Central Africa, the existence of which seemed proved by popular belief. Lake Kúra, says Abú-l-fedá, is 1000 miles long. On its western side, near Jábi, flows the Nile of Ghánah; and at its north-eastern angle, near the capital of Kánem, the Nile of

---

18 Hají Hamed (Quart. Rev. 1820, No. 45, p. 232), among others, bears witness to the course of the Great River from the Sea of Nyffé to Egypt by Kachenah and Kano. Capt. Lyon's informant, however (Lyon's Trav. p. 142), traces the stream from Funda to Katagum, while Ben Yusuf, Hornemann's son (Denham, I. p. 334), and Mohammed Miṣri (Jour. Roy. Inst. 1823, p. 5) are equally positive in making it flow through Adamawa. Much has been said of the unanimity of the natives in connecting the waters of Lake Chad with the River Chadda, but they agree only in the vague outlines of a theory, not in facts; they are unanimous in making the Kowára flow into the Chad, and not the Chad into the Kowára.

Egypt issues from it. Here it is apparent that the lake Kúra described by Ibn Fáṭimah, the lake Kúra, or river Kowára or Quorra of the present day, is supposed to be united with Lake Chad, and that it gives its name to the great inland sea, thus formed by theory. The lake Kúra of Yáḳút and Abú-l-fedá derives its origin from facts arbitrarily combined and expanded; it owes its magnitude to the distance between the waters thus connected together, and its name to the western portion of them, the river Kowára or Quorra.

Some of the systematic Arab geographers divided Africa into three great regions, viz. Genéwah, Kaúkaú or Karkar, and Habesh or Abyssinia; others into four, Genéwah, Nubia, Habesh, and Zinj.[219] Genéwah, or the western division, was disproportionately enlarged, owing to the protraction of the Great River, the incurvations of which were overlooked, and because, in speculative geography, the known has a constant tendency to encroach upon and narrow the limits of the unknown. Zinj, on the other hand, must have been diminished, since Ibn Baṭúṭah believed Sofálah to be but a month's journey distant from Yúfi (Núfí), on the left bank of the Great River, before it turned towards Nubia. The centre of the continent, where those divisions met, was occupied by Lake Kúra, whence issued the Niles of Ghánah, Egypt, and Maḳdishó. The shores of the lake were inhabited by the Demdem or (in the Arabicised plural) Demádem, who therefore stood, as occupants of the remote interior, in a defined relation with the coasts to which those rivers descended. When Arab writers, therefore, in speaking of the eastern coast of Africa, state that the interior is possessed by the Demádem, who invaded Abyssinia and Nubia in the early part of the thirteenth century, it it obvious that they speak the language of system (the name Demdem or Demádem being in reality unknown on the eastern coast), and hypothetically trace the

---

219 The author of the Kitábu-l-Járafiah divides Africa into three parts, one of which is Karkar: Shehabeddin (Not. et Extr. tom. II. p. 156), adopting the same division, writes Kaúkaú. The division into four parts is frequently referred to by Marmol (tom. I. pp. 18, 21, 31), who follows probably Ibn Gezzar.

course of the invaders from the shores of Lake Kúra and the sources of the great rivers.[20]

There is no injustice done to the Arabs in thus ascribing altogether to theory a positive statement made by many of their best authors. It is in the highest degree improbable, that with little or no knowledge of the various Black nations inhabiting the eastern coast of Africa, they should have had any accurate acquaintance with the remote interior: and besides, the acquiescence in system here imputed to them, is no greater than must have inevitably arisen from the imperfect state of their knowledge. Little more than a century ago, European geographers represented Abyssinia as occupying nearly a fourth of the African continent; on its eastern borders they placed a great lake, from which issued the Egyptian Nile, and all the great rivers of Southern Africa.[21] The maps of Africa of that date exhibit less vacant space than they do at the present day. The improvement of geography, with respect to that quarter of the globe, has consisted chiefly in reducing what is known within its proper limits. Distant nations were of course as easily brought together and united as distant countries. The different African tribes which, in the course of the sixteenth century, devastated the widely-separate coasts of Sierra Leone, of Angola, and of Melinda, were, by a sweeping generalization, all supposed to be one and the same people, and were furthermore identified with the

---

[20] El Bekrí probably wrote Remrem; though El Idrísí, copying him, writes Demdem; the latter author names also the Lemlem. Ibn Sáíd may be conjectured to have written Yemyem, but the doubtful text of the MSS. leaves the point undecided. Abú-l-fedá mentions not only the Demdem, but also the Nemnem, which latter people he places south of Saharte (the most eastern district of Tígré in Abyssinia) and of Samhar (the Dankali coast), and consequently in what is now called the Taltal country. All those names, Nemnem excepted, refer to the same people.

[21] In the maps of Forlani and others of the sixteenth century, the Nile, Zaire, Cuama, and Spirito Santo, were all made to flow from Lake Zambere. Sanson however (1650) allowed that lake no outlet towards the east, but Hollar (London, 1667) still joined the river of Kílwah with Lake Zaflan, which, as well as Lake Zambere, was connected with the Nile. In all these maps Abyssinia extended to lat. 18° S. Delisle was the first who reformed these absurdities.

Agows and Gallas of Abyssinia.[222] Vestiges of these ideas still remain in our treatises of geography, and in some of the latest maps, nor is the system of thinking from which they emanated yet quite obsolete.[23] But the close resemblance of European theories respecting the mysterious interior of Africa to those of the Arabs, is strikingly manifest in the following words of the Portuguese historian, Da Couto:—"About the year 1570, a horde of barbarians, like locusts, issued from the heart of Ethiopia, from the great lake whence flows the Cuama, the Zaire, the Rhapta, and the Nile."[24]—Here then we

---

[222] Labat (Rel. Hist. de l'Ethiopie Occidentale, II. p. 90), copying, but not faithfully, Cavazzi de Montecucoli, states, with surprising coolness, as matter of history, the supposed origin of the Jagas in the country of the Monoemugi (Monomoézi). The country of the Jagas, that is to say, of the chieftains so entitled, lies immediately behind Angola, perhaps not above 250 miles from the sea coast, and there is nothing in the history of their followers calculated to show that they come from the remote interior. Andrew Battel, who was seized on the coast and carried off by the Jagas, with whom he spent above a year, says (Purchas' Pilgrims, II. p. 973), that they told him they come from Sierra Leone. This absurd statement shows that Battel had got into his head some of the geographical speculations of his day. The Jesuit Sandoval (Hist. de Ethiop. p. 48) thus abridges the information of the missionaries: "About ninety years back, a nation called in their own country Gangédes, in Congo, Jagas, in Angola, Guindes, in India (Eastern Africa), Zimbas, in Ethiopia (Abyssinia), Gallas, and in Sierra Leone, Zumbas (Cumbas, in Jarric, probably for Çumbas), which name they changed for Manes, and who lived on human flesh, issued forth," &c. Finally, Anguiano (Epitome Historial &c. del Imp. Abyss. 1706, p. 8), speaking of the Agows, assures us that the names Agáo, Agag, and Giagos, or Giacos, are all the same.

[23] A writer in a popular journal, says of the Zoolus (properly Amazúla,) near Natal,—"They extend much further northward, where they are found under the names Sualies and Gallas." (Quart. Rev. Febr. 1837, p. 178.) The Arabic word Sowáḥilí means "inhabiting the coasts."

[24] The portion of Da Couto's History here quoted (Decade X. lib. 6, c. 15) has never been printed, but the Library of the British Museum possesses two MS. copies of it. The lake here referred to is called by De Barros Zambere, a name copied servilely by all succeeding writers, though it was doubtless a misprint for Zambeze. Cuama is the name given to the lower portion of the Zambeze, which river is so named according to Dos Santos (Ethiop. Orient. p. 44), because, on quitting the Great Lake, from which proceed the chief rivers of Southern Africa, it flows through a territory inhabited by a people of that name." The people alluded

have the exact counterpart of Lake Kúra and the Demdem or Demádem. The subsequent history of the horde referred to by Da Couto is taken up by other learned writers, who affect to describe its march southwards from Mombása to the Cape of Good Hope; thence to Angola, whence it spread to Sierra Leone and elsewhere: so that not even the Demádem were ever carried by conjecture so far from their native homes.[25] Thus it appears that the theories ascribed above to the Arabs, much excelled in sobriety, while they were exactly parallel in design with the geographical speculations of a later age.

The position of the kingdoms of Negroland enumerated by Arab writers having been now discussed and determined, and the efforts of Arab theorists to mould into unity and form the isolated facts before them, having been traced out, our task is at an end. The demonstration of the fact that Ghánah lay between the desert and the Great River near Tomboktú, at once reconciles with nature and probability, the history of the constant intercourse of that state with Sijilmésah. The nation whose language is spoken in the most important part of Negroland, is now brought into light. The Tekrúr have been traced from the vicinity of Silla to the eastern bank of the

---

to are the Ambios of Da Couto, the Movíza of the Portuguese of the present day, but who call themselves M'Bíza. The true name of the river, therefore (and that intended also to be given to the lake), is Zambíza. N'yassi, or *the sea*, as this lake is called by the natives (whence D'Anville's Massi, by mistake for Niassi), is commonly but erroneously designated in our maps Lake Marávi. The Marávi country, that is to say, the country in which the chieftains bear the title of Marávi, extends from the Zambíza to the Livúma behind Cape Delgado, and touches but does not encompass the lake. Da Couto, following De Barros, borrows the name Rhapta from Ptolemy. It serves to indicate eruditely rather than clearly what the Arabs call the River of Makdishó, that is, the Juba.

[25] Cavazzi de Montecucoli, a laborious and sincere writer, relates (Istorica Descrittione de tre Regni, &c. 1690, book II. c. 3) that a chief named Zimbo raised an army in Congo, with which he invaded Melinda on the opposite coast. Being there defeated, he retired towards the Cape of Good Hope, and afterwards attacked Angola, &c. Zimbo's marches equalled those of Tamerlane. The enormous exaggerations and mistakes of the Catholic Missionaries respecting the interior of Southern Africa, still retain their places in works of geography.

Kowára. The History of Málí has been made known, and the limits of that empire partially determined. It has been clearly shown that Kághó was also called Kaúkaú, but that the application of the latter name to one or more other places, further east, has caused incurable confusion. The ignorance and erroneous hypothesis of the Africans respecting the course of the Kowára, have been detected in the ancient accounts of Lake Kúra; and the limits of the positive knowledge of the Arabs have been ascertained in the fact that their theoretical geography embraced that lake, and the Demdem who inhabited its shores.

It will not be necessary to dwell here on the general harmony and widely-extended coincidence attending the conclusions arrived at in the preceding pages. A long series of inferences, each stamped with the character of likelihood, and all agreeing perfectly among themselves, yet obtained independently of one another, not by straining arbitrarily selected texts, but by eliciting and examining each author's fullest meaning, and which form together a complete whole, reconcileable not only with geographical facts, but also with that speculative mind, which in the history of human knowledge is itself an incontestible though not easily seized fact;—such a series of inferences, we say, carries with it an internal evidence of truth not easily impugned. It remains therefore only to recal attention to the chief historical revolutions brought to light in the course of our inquiries. The wars and conquests of the Morabites eventually opened the Western Desert to commercial enterprise. The impulse given by the religious enthusiasm of the same people to Tekrúr, spread rapidly through western Negroland, till at length the wave recoiling on the desert, the Ṣúṣú first, and then the people of Málí, became masters of Ghánah, and reckoned some of the Zenágah tribes among their tributaries.[226] The outlines of the history

[226] A Mandingo warrior named Abba Manca (Mança?), conquered Bambúk in the beginning of the twelfth century, and compelled its inhabitants to adopt the Mohammedan rites (Golberry, Fragmens d'un Voy. I. p. 419). Silla was one of the first converted of the negro towns; and as, in the Mandingo language, the word Silla means a way, road, pass, or ferry, and might therefore have been naturally

of Málí deserve particular attention. The establishment of extensive empires in the early stages of society, almost always give rise to a better order of things, by breaking down the obstructions to general intercourse, and allowing free scope to aspiring industry. The progress of Tekrúr eastwards, the foundation of Aghades, and the change effected by both these events in the condition of Houssa, have been already pointed out, and need not be further insisted on.[27]

It is impossible to deny the advancement of civilization in that zone of the African continent which has formed the field of our inquiry. Yet barbarism is there supported by natural circumstances with which it is vain to think of coping. It may be doubted whether, if mankind had inhabited the earth only in populous and adjoining communities, slavery would have ever existed. The Desert, if it be not absolutely the root of the evil, has, at least, been from the earliest times the great nursery of slave hunters.[28] The demoralization of the towns on the southern borders of the desert has been pointed out; and if the vast extent be considered of the region in which man has no riches but slaves, no enjoyment but slaves, no article of trade but slaves, and where the hearts of wandering thousands are closed against pity by the galling misery of life, it will be difficult to resist the conviction that the solid buttress on which slavery rests in Africa, is—The Desert.

---

employed to designate a town situate on the line of traffic, it may be conjectured that Silla belonged to the Mandingoes from the beginning. It may be here observed that the termination *boo* (see Note 48), characterizing the names of villages in Bambara, signifies a hut. (Dard. Dict. Wolofe, pp. 19, 22 ; Caillié, III. p. 301).

27 The Sultan of the Fellátah dynasty in Houssa styles himself Sultan of Tekrúr. The Fellátah conquerors of Houssa issued, in the beginning of the present century, from the province of Ader, adjoining Kábí on the north, and where they may have been long established. It is possible then that the kingdom of Tekrúr, mentioned to Niebuhr by Abdu-r-Raḥmán Aga, and also heard of by Hutchinson (Bowdich, p. 483), may have belonged to the Fellátah dynasty now dominant in Houssa.

28 The Garamantes, a Libyan nation, chased, in chariots drawn by four horses, the Ethiopian Troglodytes (Herodotus, book IV. c. 152). El Idrísí (in Jaubert's Trans. I. p. 110,) remarks that stealing children to sell them to strangers for a trifle, is a general practice in the desert, and "no one there sees harm in it."

POSTSCRIPT.

REMARKS ON HOUSSA.

THE route from the capital of Ashantí, through Gonja, to the Kowára or Quorra opposite to Yaúry, is determined as satisfactorily as can be expected from native information. Three different itineraries of that route agree in the chief points, conducting from Lake Buro, or from Salagha (which is the same as Dagwumba), through Tonuma, Jabzogho, Ghofil, Zogho, Jambodú, Suso and Kúka to Nikki, the capital of Borghú. Beyond this place is the town of Rugha, the River Wori, and the mountains over which lies the road to Sholo on the banks of lake Kúra (the Quorra). But in two of the itineraries the names Rugha, Wori, and Kúra are written Ḍugha, Woḍi, and Kúḍa.[229]

[229] One of these routes is given by Dupuis (App. 124), another by Bowdich (p. 491), and a third, translated from the original Arabic by De Sacy, is inserted in Walckenaer's Recherches (p. 453). The comparison of this last route with the fragment (No. 11) in Dupuis' Appendix (p. 135), shows that its author was Mohammed al Marrawi, the servant of Ibrahím, from whom Bowdich derived his information. The Sholo of the Itineraries is the Sooloo of Lander (Exped. to the Niger, II. p. 28), who means by the expression "the left bank of the river," the bank on his left hand, and contra-distinguishes it from the east bank, on which his horses were. The systematic substitution of *d* for *r* by the natives of a part of Houssa, is manifest from these itineraries. The words Barrabadi and Gamhadi, for Beráberi and Kombori, are other instances of the same change; and probably the savage and naked people called Maradi, said to inhabit the country between Kachenah and Guber (Lyon, p. 140), are no other than the Marrí, or people of Marra. The deposed King of Houssa lives in Maradi (Lander, Sec. Exped. p. 63, 153). Dupuis describes a route from Salagha, a little eastward of north, to what he calls the great

From Sholo the route conducts by Kambashi, Ghúnti, and Yendukka to Kachenah in twenty-five days. Other native routes, passing northwards of this through the mountainous country of Fagh, cross the river at Gongo (*i. e.* the ferry,) to Múrí (Múli), and then proceed through Kábí, over the Gulbi Kambaji to Raka, and thence through Kotú-n-kúra to Marki, and crossing the hills near Surami to Kachenah. The Gulbi Kambaji (river of Kambaji) of Dupuis, it has been already observed, is the same as the Gambarou (Kamba-roa, or Kamba water) of Bowdich. The latter writer places to the north of it, Mallowa, Kallaghee (Kilghí), Barrabadi (Berâberi), and Kachenah. On the south side of his Gambarou, or between it and the Quorra, he sets Gauw, Gamhadi (Kombori), Fillani, Goubirri, Zamfarra, Yaoura, and Noufí. If a partial error in the position of Mallowa be allowed for, and a more decided one in the case of Gauw, it will be evident that the river dividing the countries here enumerated is the Quorrama, or river of Kábí.[30]

Mohammed Masíní, describing the Kowára, says, "this great river issues from the Mountain of the Moon; and

---

city of Andari, respecting which there is room for some curious conjectures. But it will be sufficient for the present to remark that his Andari عنظر (Itin. No. 6) and Fadaly فضلى (No. 10), on the importance of both of which places he dwells with complacency, are in reality one and the same.

[30] For the Gharanti and Yendoto of Dupuis, Ghúnti (the Gonde of Clapperton) and Yendukka (the Yendukwa of that traveller, and Yendakka of Lyon,) are here read, the change in Arabic writing being extremely easy. The name Kandashy, which Mr. Dupuis gives to a part of Houssa, originated in a mistake. He joined the word Dúshi, signifying the hills or mountains, to a part of some preceding word. Marina, Kandashy, ought to be Markí, and Dúshi, or the hills. Mr. Dupuis continues, "Great Souy is the name of the adjoining country; there is also another Souy, where the water is very broad, and bears the name of Boromi Mághami." For Souy سوو in this place we must read Surmi سرم, a name variously altered into Solan, Zulami, Zurmie and Zirmie. The situation of Surmi, or rather Surami the less, is pointed out by Clapperton (Sec. Exped. p. 164). Lander crossed the river of Makamie (Mághami). The word Boromi apparently signifies river, in some dialect the use of which extends into Bornú and Kánem.

what we know of it is, that it comes from Sookan (Sókaí) to Kiya (Kiyaú, the Gauw of Bowdich), to Kabi, to Yaouri, to Boossa, to Wawa, and to Noofee; but in that place there is another river that springs from Zirmá, to Ghoober, to Zeffra, to Kory or Koora, and then enters Noofee; its name is Kaduna. On the north of it Kanbari lies; on the east is Kory; on the south are Cankan and Kafath; and on the west is Bassoa or Bashwa (Busawa, the territory of Busá). About the centre of it is the kingdom of Noofee, with that of Abyou (Abbiwa)."[231]

The river here described under the name of Kaduna, as running first northwards from Zirmá to Guber, and then southwards to Núfí, is apparently the same described by Clapperton in these words: "This stream rises only a day's journey in the mountains or hills south of Guari, runs through part of Zamfrá, and divides in one part the states of Katongkora and Guari, and enters into the Kodonia in Nyffé." The Kaduna or Kadunia enters the Kowára in the vicinity of Raka and Rabba, perhaps a little above the latter place. According to the native accounts, it is during part of the year a great river, navigated in canoes made of a single trunk of a tree, yet large enough to carry nine horses, but in the summer it is quite dry.[32]

---

[231] The Cankan of Mohammed Masíní is probably the Ghana-ghanah of Wargee. (Asiat. Journ. 1823, vol. XVI. p. 23.)

[32] There is, no doubt, some difficulty in believing that the mouth of the Kadunia is above Rabba, when Lander states so clearly that it is below Fofo; yet a MS. sketch of the route from Kano to the Kowára in Núfí, drawn by Clapperton from native information, places it between Rabba and Leechee, and directly opposite to Raka. Bakani, the capital, is one day from the mouth of the river; it seems to lie directly in the road from Kanó and Zegzeg to Raka and Katunga (Hertha, July 1827, Geogr. Zeit. pp. 11, 14). From one of Clapperton's MS. vocabularies, communicated to me by my invaluable friend, the Rev. G. C. Renouard, it would appear that the word Kaduna, in the Houssa language, signifies *little*. If this be correct, which appears very questionable, there are probably several rivers of that name. Here it may be remarked, that when Dupuis (pt. II. p. 100) speaks of Saghona, the capital of Yekoo (Ako or Yariba), he means Raka, which is also called Saguda (Clapp. p. 60).

The country called by Mohammed Masíní, Kory or Koora (Kúra), is either the Guari of the maps, or else Kotú-n-kúra. The resemblance of this name to that of the great river (Lake Kúra) deserves attention. It appears probable that the natives of Houssa name the Great River from what they conceive to be its sources in their own country, tracing it from Kowára (the Guari of Clapperton), through Zamfara and Kábí, down to the sea of Kúra or of Núfí.[33] Hence it is not surprising, that, while Ibn Sáíd mentions Kúra among the kingdoms of Negroland, Yaḳút and Abú-l-fedá should apply that name to the great water which there received the Nile of Ghánah.

---

[33] Clapperton (Sec. Exped. p. 232) says that the capital of Zegzeg is called Quorra. He probably means to speak of the town which he elsewhere calls Guari, but the name of which, in the native maps brought home by him, is written Ḳowárah. When he speaks of Kóra (p. 133), he appears to have in view the capital of Kotú-n-Kúra. This name is, through obvious mistake, written Kotunfauda in Bello's map. Kotú is a name of frequent occurrence, as in Kotú-n-karafi (in the maps Cuttum Curraffee), "where there is a copper mine" (Bello in Denh. Disc. II. p. 451). Karafi means metal in general. The country named Kúra is mentioned, together with Niffi and Raka, by the Kaíd ben Yusuf (Denh. Disc. I. p. 334). The slaves Boniface and Francisco agreed in representing to M. Menézes de Drummond (Hertha, pp. 13, 14), that the Kowára rises in the centre of Houssa, and that it takes its name from the country named Kuara (Kowára), through which it flows.